A Pudding Full of Plums

A Pudding Full of Plums

by

Jack Jeffery

To Joan and Duncan with kindest regards.

Jack.

The Memoir Club

© Jack Jeffery 2006

First published in 2006 by
The Memoir Club
Stanhope Old Hall
Stanhope
Weardale
County Durham

British Library Cataloguing in
Publication Data.
A catalogue record for this book
is available from the
British Library

ISBN: 1-84104-154-8

Typeset by TW Typesetting, Plymouth, Devon
Printed by CPI Bath

To my wife Deborah and
my daughters Wyn, Carole and Jill

Contents

List of Illustrations

Foreword

Jack and Deborah Jeffery are good friends of ours. My wife and I do not see them as often as we would like, but we always look forward to being with them and, when we are, we always appreciate it. Jack is challenging. Deborah is warm and full of fun. Her leeks are something special! We wish we had known them both far earlier in our lives.

This memoir is fascinating. There is something of the complete man in Jack, not least the frustrations: son, grandson, father, grandfather, music and jazz lover, pianist, cricketer, humanist, chemist, professional, public servant, businessman and activist. It is, however, the family pages which positively burst with pride. He has real roots and values them. The descriptions of his childhood and formative years in the north east are vivid. His love of his children and grandchildren is unqualified. He gives us an intimate insight into a family going through the intellectual, political and social struggles of the 1930s. Trade unionism, the Labour Party, communism, the Spanish Civil War, and principled atheism clearly left their mark on Jack in his wise approach to all that followed. The war years and national service are seen from an interesting perspective. It is no surprise that, in his more recent years, Jack has returned to a brim full life in his beloved north east, not least a significant role in Newcastle University, and internationally to a major part in the humanist movement.

Jack is consistently loyal to people, principles and places alike. He has a gentle but tough integrity. He is never naive. He takes his opportunities and is not a bad hand at creating them on any road he himself wants to take. Each phase of life contributes to the next. He is learning all the time and the reader cannot help but learn with him. The years in the National Coal Board and the water industry illustrate his commitment to public service and the values of his forebears. The story he tells of the improvised privatisation by stages of the water industry is worthy of our national archives. It brings out another characteristic in his whimsical sense of humour. He is a central player and throws himself into it all with skill and vigour. Indeed, in material terms, he clearly benefits considerably. And yet there is always the sense that this is the professional Jack and not the deeper, more profound, community orientated and involuntarily obstinate man of the humanitarian left he really remains. He leaves the impression that he lent himself to the success of a rather special sector of capitalism but never totally gave himself to its under-lying philosophy.

There is something just a little enigmatic in all this. And the equation has
another element: his cheerful inability to avoid being drawn into one high
office after another in professional, civic and sporting institutions and
societies, as well as organisations devoted to the future wellbeing of
humanity. It is almost an addiction, but one from which the rest of us have
gained invaluable benefit.

This is the story of an exceptional man who has made, and continues to
make, a powerful contribution to society; but it is also an honest personal
account of the internal challenges and dilemmas encountered by him and
how they were faced and answered. It is a very interesting read. Enjoy it!

FRANK JUDD
Lord Judd of Portsea
Thackthwaite, Cockermouth, Cumbria
July 2006

Acknowledgements

When I was invited to write a memoir of my life, I realised that it would be a significant undertaking but the true scale of the project only emerged gradually. Even though I've relied almost entirely on my memory, it has taken a great deal of time spread over several years so I must begin by thanking my wife, Deborah, for her love and support, not just in the writing of this book but throughout all the tasks that I've taken on. Thanks also to my family generally, daughters, sons-in-law and grandchildren. They have all shared many ups and a few downs with me and are a source of great pride and love to me.

The foreword by Lord Judd of Portsea is typically generous and I am truly grateful to him for his kind words. I must also thank all the many friends with whom I've worked during my career in the coal, water and waste management industries and in the voluntary sector, as well as cricketing friends. Many are named in the book, many are not, but I'm grateful to all of them. My thanks also to the many friends who have helped me throughout my life, agreeing with me and disagreeing with me but always remaining true friends – not quite the definition of Mark Twain quoted at the beginning of Chapter 6.

I have borrowed the title of the book from a line by W S Gilbert in *The Gondoliers*. The quotations beginning each chapter are included as tributes to some of my favourite writers and artists.

Finally, my sincere thanks go to the staff of The Memoir Club for suggesting the book and for their encouragement and special thanks to my editor, Dr Jennifer Soutter. Her help and her patience with my last minute re-drafting have been invaluable.

Jack Jeffery
June 2006

CHAPTER 1

Childhood, family and early influences

The Moving Finger writes; and, having writ,
Moves on: nor all your Piety nor Wit,
Shall lure it back to cancel half a Line,
Nor all your Tears wash out a Word of it.

The Rubáiyát of Omar Khayyám
Rendered into English Verse by Edward Fitzgerald

'I MIND AS IF IT WERE YESTERDAY my first sight of the man' is the first
sentence of *Prester John*, one of many John Buchan adventure stories
that I loved as a boy. Those few words are amongst my clearest
memories of my primary schooldays that began in March 1935 at
Pickering Nook Council Junior Mixed School, near Stanley, in
County Durham. The school had perhaps sixty or seventy pupils and
three teachers. Miss Purdy taught the 'Babies' and Standard 1 and
Miss Jefferson taught Standard 2 and Standard 3. By 1939 I had
reached Standard 4, which was taught, jointly with Standard 5, (the
top class), by the Headmaster, William Simpson. Bill Simpson was an
excellent teacher and one of the earliest people to influence me
outside my family. One day he began to read *Prester John* with us. I
remember him starting by saying, 'It's important to begin any piece
of writing with a sentence that catches the reader's attention from the
start. *Prester John* is a really good example'. So it seems right to begin
these memories with a tribute to my first headmaster.

My time at Pickering Nook School was happy, especially when I
reached the top group taught by Bill Simpson. He always encouraged
me but also knew when to call a halt. As a teacher, he had that special
quality of making people want to please him that later in my life I
recognised as the most important common factor in all of the better
managers that I met. On the occasions when I did something wrong
and he found out, I was far from happy, even though I can't
remember ever seeing him really lose his temper.

Corporal punishment wasn't uncommon at Pickering Nook
School and I was from time to time on the receiving end of Miss

Author's maternal great-grandparents

Jefferson's leather strap and Mr Simpson's cane. We all hated to be punished and in principle, I agree with the current view of such methods. Certainly, it would be impossible to re-introduce them now. But I'm not sure that it did us any harm and like everything else, I think that it has to be considered in the wider context of the social attitudes of the time.

One of the highlights of the school year was the annual school trip to Whitley Bay. We all used to pay a few pence each week to cover the cost, which I think added to our excited anticipation of the event. When the great day arrived, we couldn't wait to board the buses and when we saw the sea, it was a wonderful feeling.

Our mothers provided us with enough food for a week and we had a little pocket money to spend on ice cream and in the Spanish City fairground. At the end of the day, we had to find our bus from amongst what seemed like hundreds of buses parked near the seafront. Then, we were on our way back to Pickering Nook singing, 'Show me the way to go home' with our own words and feeling very witty.

I was an only child, born on 10 March 1930 in a maternity home in Yarm Road, Stockton-on-Tees in County Durham at a time when my parents were living in Yorkshire, just across the river from Stockton at Thornaby on Tees. As a sport-mad boy, I once pointed out to my mother that she had made it impossible for me to play cricket for Yorkshire by crossing the Tees to Stockton for my birth.

My mother was what used often to be described as *petite*. She was almost five feet tall, wore size three shoes and was very pretty. She had been born Elsie Carr on 30 May 1905 and my father was Philip Jeffery, born on 27 September 1904. Elsie and Phil were married in Lanchester Register Office in County Durham on 25 May 1928. Their early years of marriage were spent in the Stockton and Richmond, North Yorkshire areas. Apart from living at Thornaby, they also had a house at nearby Norton and lived for a time at Gilling West, an idyllic village near Richmond in Yorkshire.

Phil had 'served his time' as a plasterer and in those difficult days, they moved wherever there was building work to be found. By the time I was three, my father had become foreman in his brother Bob's plastering contracting firm and we had moved to Clough Dene, near Tantobie in County Durham, to live in the large house there that was owned by my paternal grandfather, John Jeffery. Although some new houses have since been built there, Clough Dene is still really no more than a hamlet, with no facilities like a shop or a pub but it was a wonderful place to grow up. The house where we lived stands on land that slopes steeply both at the back and to the side in about two and a half acres of land, then used as a market garden and poultry farm. There were trees to climb and a strip of grass where cousins, friends and I used to play cricket and football.

Great-grandfather Jeffery had been a tin miner in Cornwall, where my grandfather, John Jeffery, was born in December 1865. He and his parents moved to County Durham when he was a boy. His father

Grandfather, Alderman John Jeffery

was probably looking for work in the coalmines as a result of problems in the Cornish tin industry at that time. My grandfather Jeffery lived until 1956 so I was able to spend a lot of time with him and he was a major influence on my early development. I remember him describing how he had 'gone down the pit' at Seaham Harbour at the age of twelve for ten pence per day, earning five shillings a week (25 pence) for a six-day week. In his late teens he became a Methodist local preacher, as he told me, preaching 'hell and damnation'. At about the same time, he joined the fledgling Independent Labour Party, (the ILP), and came across many fellow Methodists there but also met a number of what he used to describe to me as 'militant atheists'. John Jeffery soon joined the ranks of the militant atheists.

In the mid-thirties, I grew up in a house where my father read the left of centre *News Chronicle* on weekdays and *The Observer* on Sundays and my grandfather took the Labour supporting *Daily Herald*, the communist *Daily Worker* and the Co-operative movement paper,

Author as a child

Reynolds News, on Sunday, as well as the secularist paper, the *Freethinker* every week. It was far from a conventional political upbringing!

By that time, John Jeffery was an official of the Durham Miners Association (later to become part of the National Union of Mineworkers) and worked nearby as Checkweighman at Hobson Colliery, virtually joined to Pickering Nook and a mile or so up the hill from Burnopfield. Political debate took place at Clough Dene regularly when I was a boy, but most particularly over supper on Sunday evenings. That was when people of many different opinions would gather to put the world right around a large mahogany table groaning with my grandmother's cold meats, meat and potato pies, fruit tarts and home-made cakes. I wasn't normally included in the supper but regularly managed to be somewhere around to hear the arguments. These were usually about politics or religion. Frequently the subjects overlapped and sometimes the discussion became rather heated.

In addition to a poultry farm and market garden with several large greenhouses, there was a vinery and my grandparents kept a few pigs at Clough Dene. In the spring, we sold plants grown in the greenhouses and 'hardened off' in cold frames. We grew various vegetables including cabbages, cauliflowers and carrots, but I think that our biggest trade was in leek plants. The counties of Durham and Northumberland were, and still remain, famous for their leek shows and it gives me great pleasure that after my retirement and return to the north-east, my London-born wife, Deborah, has taken up showing leeks with enthusiasm and more than a little success. In fact, in 2001, she won the cup for the best leek in the show and in the same year was elected to become the first woman Chairman of our village Leek Club, the Feathers Inn Leek Club, a considerable honour.

There was an orchard at Clough Dene with plum, apple and pear trees and there were blackcurrants, gooseberries, raspberries, and strawberries to be picked in summer. We also grew tomatoes, cucumbers and rhubarb in the greenhouses and everyone was expected to help without any formal method of payment. For me, the two worst jobs were thinning out the grapes in the vinery and picking frozen Brussels sprouts. I hated picking sprouts but perhaps thinning grapes was even worse. It was such a slow job and involved standing on a stepladder working with a pair of scissors overhead and getting a severe stiff neck in the process. I expect that my grandfather, John Jeffery, the well-known socialist, saw it all as a kind of co-operative, but there were those among my older cousins who thought that they saw a degree of hypocrisy in the system that he operated! I probably spent more time than most with my grandfather and was fascinated by his stories and as a boy, was just happy to be accepted by him. As an official of his trade union, the Durham Miners Association and a County Councillor, he often attended conferences and I remember his stories of visits to faraway places like Bournemouth.

At the end of the General Strike in 1926, my grandfather took out a mortgage on the house at Clough Dene and he and my grandmother went off to Canada and the United States for, I was told, a six-month holiday. Both grandparents told me many stories of their voyage across the Atlantic and their visits to Montreal, Toronto, Detroit and so on. It must have seemed to everyone a remarkable thing to do at such a time. I loved having a cold beef sandwich with my grandmother and hearing her stories.

My grandfather was a man of strongly-held opinions and in my experience, never plagued by self-doubt. If we, as boys, caught people stealing from the market garden, my grandfather was as likely as not to send them away with a bunch of grapes from the vinery or half a dozen eggs. He wasn't always consistent in matching actions to beliefs but how many of us are? My family have been known to draw comparisons with my grandfather when discussing my character and behaviour.

When the war started in 1939, we knew that there would be a problem in getting coal to feed the massive boiler that provided hot water to heat the greenhouses. There was a drift mine in the field next to our garden so we worked out that there was likely to be a coal scam outcropping half way up the hill in the garden facing the house. I remember some vague talk of mineral rights and royalties, but the general view in the family was that such legal niceties arose from an unfair economic system and should be ignored in such a crisis.

Therefore, a small drift was driven into the hillside with the entrance screened by bushes. The mine eventually extended maybe fifty or sixty yards underground and some time later, there was some concern when a pitfall appeared in the field next to the garden. The problem was that the farmer might apply for compensation from the local coal-owner. If that were to happen, it would not take the surveyors long to establish that the pitfall was caused by an unofficial mine. However, nothing ever came of it and Clough Dene continued to contribute to the war effort by supplying food grown in heated greenhouses to Stanley market.

My grandfather Jeffery was a man of great enthusiasm and that sometimes made him vulnerable to advertising. During the war, one of the slogans used by the Government was 'Dig for Victory' and everyone was encouraged to bring under cultivation land that was lying fallow. One weekend, my grandfather saw a newspaper advertisement for a pig harness and he immediately saw that this offered the opportunity of a double benefit. A pig could be tethered on land on a steep hill in the garden at Clough Dene that had never been cultivated. The pig would feed mainly on the vegetation growing there, so we would finish up with a piece of land 'broken in' for cultivation and a pig to kill for pork and bacon. The pig harness arrived and my grandfather and I went off to put it on one of the pigs. It was not easy! To a casual observer, we would have seemed a strange pair, my grandfather about seventy-five years old while I was about ten.

The first step was to drive an iron post into the ground in the centre of the land to be broken in. Grandfather said, 'You hold the post steady and I'll drive it in with the mell'. It sounded straightforward, (although I remember thinking that it sounded a little too much like the old joke about 'When I nod my head, hit it') and I held the iron post while my grandfather attempted to drive it into the ground. Unfortunately, the ground was dry and extremely hard and the hammer rarely seemed to hit the post squarely, so I felt myself to be in considerable danger, but eventually, the post was in place and miraculously, I hadn't suffered any injury. My grandfather then said 'I'll hold the pig while you slip the harness over its head.'

A pig is a large and powerful animal. Therefore, my grandfather did not find it easy to hold the pig's head still and some time elapsed and much energy was expended before we managed to get the harness around the pig's shoulders. The next step was to connect one end of a chain to the harness on the pig and the other end to the post. Which to do first?

Both approaches were fraught with difficulty. Somehow, we managed to make the connection and stood back to admire the results of all our efforts. As soon as it was released, the pig charged off down the hill and the post so strenuously driven into the ground survived in that position for about half a second. The next thing we knew, the pig was running along the road towards Tantobie, dragging behind it the post still attached by the chain to the harness. I remember my grandfather running after it while I just collapsed in fits of laughter. It was like a scene from a P G Wodehouse story about Lord Emsworth's prize pig, the Empress of Blandings.

My father, Phil, was the tenth child of John and Elizabeth Jeffery and his parents were both approaching forty when he was born. His young sister, Derry, sadly died of diphtheria at the age of eleven before I was born, leaving my father as the youngest surviving child. My father was a quiet and intelligent man. He did not inherit his father's passion for debate, but generally shared his views on politics and religion. Phil was a good club cricketer and I spent many happy days in the late thirties watching my father play cricket at Tantobie, where he was first team captain. My mother was also part of the family cricket ritual because she was one of the group of women who 'did the teas' every other week.

My father encouraged me to play cricket and showed me endlessly how to play the back foot defensive stroke, a key requirement on the local wickets, which often were not very good in those days. I can still hear him saying, 'Get your left elbow up and your right foot across and back towards the stumps'. It was quite some time before I realised that it wasn't always a good idea to play back and that there were judgments to be made about when and how to play forward and when to play back. I think that in those days, my father's main motivation in coaching me was maybe to lessen the risk of my being hit by the ball.

Reading was one of my father's great passions, especially the writings of authors such as Joseph Conrad, Bret Harte, Jack London and Upton Sinclair and the poetry of A E Housman. It was easy for me to recognise, even as a child, the challenge to the nineteenth and early twentieth century economic and social systems implicit in the writings of such authors. I think that maybe the adventurous nature and affirmed socialism of Jack London represented in some ways the man that my father would have liked to be. On the other hand, unlike Jack London, Phil Jeffery had no wish to drink and Jack London's racism would have horrified my father, but I don't think that many knew of that aspect of London's character at that time. While still at Pickering Nook primary school, my father gave me a copy of *The Jungle*, by Upton Sinclair and told me that I should read it. I still remember the horror I felt at the inhumanity of conditions in the meat packing factory in Chicago that it described.

One of my father's most treasured possessions was a leather-bound copy of the *Rubáiyát of Omar Khayyám*, which my mother gave him in 1928 soon after their marriage, and which is now a special reminder of my parents in my own collection of books. So, partly as a tribute to my parents and partly because it has always been special to me, this chapter opens with one of my favourite verses from the *Rubáiyát*.

My father had many outstanding abilities, among them his skill at solving crosswords and he used to complete *The Observer* crossword in less than half an hour every Sunday morning. He didn't say a lot to me but what he said, I remembered. For instance, I recall walking our dog with my father just after I'd heard that I'd passed the scholarship examination at the age of eleven and was looking forward to going to Alderman Wood Secondary School. In a completely unemotional way, he said to me, 'I don't agree with the way the world's run but I know that I'm not going to change it, so I want you to have every chance to make the best of your ability in your life.' He smiled and went on, 'I'm only a beer teetotaller, not a champagne teetotaller', quoting from Bernard Shaw (another of his favourite writers) in his play, *Candida*.

As well as believing that socialism was the right and fair way in which to organise society, my mother and father were both opposed to prejudice, whether based on skin pigments, religion or any other factor and one of their heroes was Paul Robeson, the great American bass baritone. My mother and father admired Paul Robeson as one of the great singers of his generation and as a socialist who had become accepted throughout the world in spite of the enormous difficulties he had faced as a result of racist laws and behaviour, especially in his own country of the United States. Marion Anderson was another great black American singer in a similar mould. We had a pre-war recording of Marion Anderson singing the aria 'Softly Awakes my Heart' from Saint-Saens' opera *Samson and Delilah* that was one of my favourites.

Writing of her childhood in the Introduction to her book *An Intelligent Person's Guide to Ethics*, (Duckworth, 1998), Mary Warnock wrote, 'Though we may often have behaved badly, there is no doubt that we wanted to be good'. That sums up how I remember feeling as a child, and is, maybe, a fair description of me to this day. How that feeling arose is not clear to me. Maybe, as Mary Warnock suggests, we all share it. But I think that for me, part of it came from the fact that most of us in the Jeffery family rejected the contradictions implicit in the idea of an omnipresent, omniscient and benevolent God. That sometimes seemed to mean that we had to demonstrate that we did not need the commandments of such a God to define our morality and ethics.

Much later, in the sixth form at grammar school, I began to read a little about the ideas of Plato and Aristotle on rationality and morality. I still struggle with trying to understand the contradictions in human behaviour. Problems such as why some people usually behave in ways that the majority see as good while a few behave regularly in a way that the majority see as morally bad.

Author's father

Sartre said that each man has within him the seeds of his own destruction. I think that introduces the related question of why people often act in ways contrary to their self-interest, not for ethical reasons, but to achieve consistency with their self-image. In my managerial career, as well as socially, I often felt that behaviour that seemed illogical could be explained perfectly reasonably in terms of the self-image of the person concerned.

At about the time war broke out in September 1939, little building was taking place and my father was unemployed. Then he managed to get work for a few weeks issuing the new Identity Cards that everyone received on the outbreak of war. Sometimes, I went with him and I have a clear memory of walking with him in the rain up a hill near Stanley singing a song of 1939 made popular, I think, by Flanagan and Allan, called 'The Umbrella Man' – pronounced in the song as 'any umberellas to fix today?'

Although my father was thirty-five years old in September 1939, I thought that he might have to join the army, but when he had his medical examination, he was classified as Grade 4, the lowest grade. My mother and I were pleased that he was going to stay with us but were worried about his health. He was told at one point that he was suffering from pernicious anaemia and I became really worried about him when I overheard a conversation between my mother and an aunt in which it was clear that they thought that my father was unlikely to survive for more than a few years. Eventually, just after the war, a new family doctor diagnosed the problem as severe haemorrhoids and after an operation for their removal at the then Dryburn Hospital in Durham his health slowly began to improve.

For a time during the war, my father, along with many other members of the building trade, was a member of the Rescue Service, part of the Air Raid Precautions system set up by the government known as ARP. Later, he worked as a storekeeper for the Home Guard at Stanley. Once the war in Europe ended in May 1945, the Home Guard fairly soon ceased to exist and once again, my father was out of work. His health made it impossible for him to consider going back to plastering but in 1946, he succeeded in his application for the job of Caretaker at Stanley Grammar School. He supervised a team of cleaners and his only real physical stress came from keeping the coke-fired boiler working. A pleasant, detached stone-built house next to the school went with the job and this meant leaving Clough Dene, which, for all its advantages, had always been my grandfather's house and never really our home.

I was then sixteen years old and for me, it was a great move. I'd always lived in a place that isolated me from most of my friends and so had been well away from where the action was, but I was now right in the centre of things. In the sixth form, we began to form groups with similar interests such as music and especially, jazz. The Essoldo cinema in Stanley became a favourite venue for Saturday nights out because, unlike the Pavilion and the Albert Hall, (the other two cinemas in Stanley at that time) the Essoldo had double seats along the back row of the balcony.

In those days, there were two separate 'houses' and two or three of our gang would join the queue early for the second house. By the time first house finished, there might have been between a dozen and twenty of us at the front of the queue for second house but I can't remember any of those behind us complaining. For most of us, the object of the exercise was to be able to grab one of those double seats in the back row to develop our latest relationship. Living at the

School House also meant that it was much easier to meet my friends and maybe to take a girl-friend home afterwards than it would have been living at Clough Dene.

The School House quickly became the place where all my friends gathered every Sunday evening to listen to records and talk and enjoy supper with my mother and father. People like Jack Garfoot and Margaret Vince, who celebrated their golden wedding in 2002; Sam Hunter and Norma Suddick (for some reason always known as 'Squeak') and many others. Sam and Norma later married and emigrated to Canada, Norma sadly dying in the autumn of 2003. Esmee Slattery was another of the group who liked jazz and she qualified as a tax inspector, later becoming a partner in the accountancy firm of Price Waterhouse in Newcastle. My mother's Sunday suppers became as legendary among my group as those of my grandmother had been in earlier times at Clough Dene and with similar menus. There were meat and potato plate pies and leek pasties as well as fruit tarts and cakes. But there was never any alcohol. It was never mentioned and as far as I know, none of us even thought about it in those days. The availability of beer and spirits had been restricted during the war and my mother and father were teetotal, as were my grandparents at Clough Dene so alcohol wasn't part of my culture.

At the age of sixteen or seventeen, it never occurred to any of us to go to a pub and even when I began my National Service in the RAF, I rarely drank anything alcoholic. My grandfather's attitude to alcohol was that held by many socialists at that time. He thought that it was one of the ways in which the capitalists kept the proletariat from thinking about the unfairness in society. His view of alcohol also had obvious parallels with the anti-drink proselytising of Methodists and the Salvation Army but that didn't stop my grandfather from seeing those bodies as bigoted! That was one reason for the popularity of George Bernard Shaw's *Major Barbara* among the Jeffery family at Clough Dene. When it was made into a film in, I think, 1939, starring Wendy Hiller, we all had to go to the cinema to see it.

I gradually became aware of an interesting paradox. John Jeffery shared the views of the Methodists and the Salvation Army on alcohol but he saw both alcohol and religion as 'the opium of the people'. In time, I began to understand that while many of the early socialists had been Methodists, some had been atheists and my grandfather had taken ideas from both groups and then adapted them over the years into his own set of beliefs and principles.

My mother, Elsie, was the elder of two daughters of Matthew and Elizabeth Carr. Matthew was a boot and shoemaker and as a girl, Elizabeth had been 'in service' at Thornley Hall, near Rowlands Gill in County Durham before her marriage to Matthew. There were four children, Elsie, Grace, George and Billy. Grace married Michael Wynn and they had five daughters, Pat, Noreen (who later changed her name to Honor), Dorothy, Margaret and Joyce. George and his wife Doris had two children, Alan and Helen, but Billy married fairly late in life and had no children.

Uncle Mick and Auntie Grace moved to the London area in the thirties when Michael got a good job at Elstree Film Studios. He became responsible for building film sets and I believe that there was some suggestion that my father played a part in getting Michael the union card he required to be appointed at Elstree. Grace and Mick had a life-style very different from ours. For example, they had a telephone and a large Armstrong-Siddeley car and I remember being taken before the war to London for a holiday sitting in the 'dicky seat' at the back. On that trip, we stopped at Hatfield and my father took a short pleasure flight in a tiny aeroplane. I think that was the only flight that my father made in the whole of his life. In spite of their life-style (or perhaps more likely, because of it), Grace was often short of money and I recall a few appeals to my mother for help. I had difficulty in understanding the logic of someone (in my eyes) well off seeking help from someone much worse off.

At the height of the blitz in 1940/41, my cousins Pat, Noreen and Dorothy escaped from the bombs by coming to live with us at Clough Dene for about a year. We all slept in the three attics at the top of the house and I recall having some mixed emotions about their presence. They had to endure a lot of leg pulling about what we all perceived as 'Cockney' accents, especially the way they pronounced 'bath' as 'barth'. But I think that they enjoyed their stay with us and they were able to continue their schooling in a relatively peaceful environment at a time when the London area was suffering bombing raids almost every night.

In the thirties, Uncle George and Auntie Doris also moved to London with their children, Alan and Helen, as did Billy. So although I had seven cousins on my mother's side, they all lived far from my home in County Durham.

Shortly before my mother's marriage, her father, Matthew Carr, died of cancer. A few years later, her mother, Elizabeth, married Ben Cox. When I was about three years old, he would say to me, 'Would you like a spoonful of pigeon's milk?' For a time, I believed him and then I realised that it was actually tinned condensed milk. I loved it. My grandparents Cox lived in Jutland Terrace in Tanfield Lea, near Clough Dene, but the Depression in the thirties led to them following Elizabeth's children Grace, George and Billy to the London area in search of work. They lived in Kenton, and later in Kingsbury, Middlesex, which became holiday venues for my parents and me.

As with my mother's family, some of my father's brothers and sisters moved away from the area, seeking work. Uncle Joe and his family moved to Derby, as did Aunt Lily and her family, before emigrating to New Zealand. I think that Joe and Aunt Lily's husband, Jack Johnston, both worked for Rolls Royce. But on my father's side, I had about twenty cousins and many of them remained in the County Durham area.

My father's eldest sister was my Auntie Jenny, a formidable woman, whose husband, Wheatley Clark, was a local civil servant. They had one son, Harry, and two daughters, Edna and Hilda, all several years older than me and all of them living alongside us in my grandfather's house at Clough Dene in the thirties. Harry was seventeen years my senior but always had time for me. He was a good athlete and all-round sportsman and after studying at Loughborough College, he became a physical training teacher. While he was at Loughborough, Harry set a new college record for the long jump. He had a succession of motorbikes, including an Ariel 1,000cc, and told me stories of seeing Stanley Woods riding his Velocette in the Isle of Man TT.

When war came, Harry had begun teaching at Seaham in County Durham and he joined the RAF, becoming a physical training instructor. He played wartime football with some great players of the time, including Stanley Matthews and Stan Mortenson. In 1944, just before a wartime international match between England and Scotland at Wembley, *Picture Post* published a feature on the coming game. It contained several pictures of Stan Matthews, later Sir Stanley, and I still have the copy that Harry gave me, autographed by Stan

Matthews and Stan Mortenson. Harry taught all his working life at a school in Seaham becoming Head in his forties. In April 2003, he celebrated his ninetieth birthday with a party at a hotel in Durham.

Harry's sister, Edna Clark, married Bobby Jones while still young and they lived in a tiny cottage at Allansford, a hamlet beautifully situated on the banks of the River Derwent near Consett. It was a favourite spot for camping and I camped there several times with friends from school. Bobby was a technician with Consett Iron Company and did not enjoy the best of reputations with the Jeffery family. He often brought me small gifts the origin of which was fairly obvious. For example, Bobby knew that I had some chemistry apparatus that I had bought by mail order from a firm in Stoke Newington, London called (I think) J N Beck. I had already experimented with making my own fireworks using chemicals bought from a pharmacist in Stanley and had acquired some notoriety by filling the house at Clough Dene with smoke and fumes one Sunday evening when my grandfather had visitors. So, knowing of my interest in science, Bobby gave me a stone bottle containing maybe 300 ml of mercury. Apart from the question of how he had

Childhood home at Clough Dene

acquired it, the health risk would now be taken extremely seriously. Quite how Bobby thought I was to use it was not clear and I have a feeling that it eventually found its way into the stock room of the chemistry laboratory at Stanley Grammar school possibly leading to some consternation if ever the teachers did a stocktaking.

Edna's sister Hilda worked for my grandfather at Clough Dene, working in the market garden, looking after the hens, collecting the eggs and selling them locally. In school holidays I sometimes helped Hilda and I have a silly memory of going with her to Swan's garage at Pickering Nook to buy paraffin and of us singing a duet of 'I don't want to set the world on fire'. Mr Swan had an American car that seemed to me to be huge. It was a Ford V8 and sometimes his son, John, would take me for a short ride in the car. That gave me an early taste of motoring luxury.

Uncle Bob, my father's boss, was the eldest son and he and Auntie Maggie lived two miles away, at Stanley, with their four daughters and one son. Before the war, Uncle Bob had a red Flying Standard car at a time when most cars were black. It seemed to me to be very exciting and completely beyond any reasonable ambition I might have.

Then there were the three sons of my father's brother John and his wife, my Aunt Polly. Ron was nine years older, Colin five years older and Harry eighteen months younger than me. They lived at Tanfield Hospital, known locally as the 'Fever Hospital' because it specialised in treatment of scarlet fever and diphtheria, and Uncle John was responsible for the maintenance of the grounds. It was about a mile from Clough Dene and I spent many happy childhood days there with my cousins. We climbed trees and played cricket on the grass tennis court provided for the nurses, while Auntie Polly pretended to be strict and spoiled us all.

The eldest son, Ron, became, like Harry Clark a kind of role model for me. Like Harry, he was a good cricketer and footballer. When the war began, he had just passed his Higher School Certificate and obtained a County Exhibition to go to university, so he went off to Sheffield in the autumn of 1939 to read geography. In 1942, having achieved an honours BA, Ron joined the army and was commissioned in the Royal Electrical and Mechanical Engineers (REME), serving in Egypt and in a gun battery at Dover, finishing the war as a Major. He then taught at Blackpool and at Spennymoor in County Durham, finishing as Deputy Head of Greencroft School near Annfield Plain. Both Harry and Ron wrote to me regularly throughout the war and influenced my development in many ways.

My father's sister, Dora, also lived nearby at Crookgate, Burnopfield, with my Uncle Sid and their son, Alan Rix, who was two years my senior. Alan was also a good sportsman and attended the neighbouring grammar school of Hookergate, near Rowlands Gill. After National Service in the RAF, Alan went to Edinburgh University where he took a degree in forestry and subsequently had a successful career with the Forestry Commission. Alan's sister had died of diphtheria at the age of two. Uncle Sid was a bus conductor for Northern Buses before and after the war, although during the war, he worked in an armaments factory at Coventry.

As a little boy, I sometimes took a bus on which Uncle Sid was the conductor. He would say, 'Where to?' without any sign of recognition. Then he would take my money, flick the lever on his ticket machine; pretend to give me a ticket and give me back my money, pretending that it was my change. I enjoyed the conspiracy, but also dreaded the possibility of an inspector getting on the bus at the next stop and catching us out. Fortunately, it didn't ever happen.

Uncle Sid was also a good card player, especially of whist and solo and he played a good game of billiards. Auntie Dora had a powerful personality with the ability to upset people from time to time. She had some famous rows in the sixties with my cousin Ron, often based on her view that the government wasn't doing enough for the pensioners. Her approach could be blunt but she was always kind to me and I still have the complete piano music of the *Lieder ohne Worte* of Mendelssohn that she herself hand bound in leather and gave me for Christmas during the war.

Another of my father's sisters, my Auntie Carrie, lived a mile away at Tantobie with my Uncle Alf and their son, Jeffery Voysey, almost exactly my age. Auntie Carrie suffered terribly from rheumatoid arthritis and I remember the joints of her hands being twisted and almost rigid. At about the end of the war, I recall that everyone was suddenly hopeful that she might be cured. We were told that she was going to be given a new wonder drug called cortisone, but whether or not that was true, she never did get any better. Auntie Carrie and Uncle Alf had a general dealer's shop in the front of their terraced house. Uncle Alf wrote poetry and drove a horse and cart around the area selling fruit and vegetables. Occasionally, I was allowed to ride the horse without my mother knowing. When I was eleven, I used to take packets of five Woodbine cigarettes from the shop and put my two pence halfpenny in the till. After a few weeks, my mother found out that I was smoking and my smoking stopped abruptly. I re-started smoking during my National Service in the RAF and then stopped permanently in 1959, soon after the publication of the first epidemiological report of the work of Sir Richard Doll linking smoking with lung cancer.

So although I had no brothers or sisters, I had plenty of older cousins around to provide me with role models as well as cousins near my own age for companionship. My childhood in the thirties was extremely happy. In addition to my cousins, I had many friends at Pickering Nook School. Boys like Ken Hogarth and Tommy Cook and girls like Alma Jackson and Linda Clark. Ken Hogarth had the best Hornby train set and Tommy Cook was a good cricketer, in spite of having to wear leg irons because of suffering from rickets, an affliction that was quite common at that time. Much later, Tommy and I played cricket against each other when he played for Burnopfield in the Tyneside Senior League.

Sometimes we all played together at Hobson and there were trees to climb and there was cricket to be played at Clough Dene. There was a cinema in Tantobie, the Regal, and there were also two cinemas in Burnopfield, the Grand and the Pavilion, and many of us used to go to the Saturday matinée at one of them. There was always a cowboy serial featuring Tom Mix, Ken Maynard, Buck Jones or the great Alsatian dog, Rin Tin Tin. Each episode always ended with the hero or heroine in a situation from which there could be no possible escape. But we all knew that if we followed the instruction to 'come back next week', we would discover that somehow, rescuers had arrived in the nick of time and all was well.

Apart from relatively minor ailments such as scarlet fever, I was generally healthy, perhaps because my mother always provided plenty of good, wholesome food. She was a great believer in the virtues of fruit, vegetables, milk and butter. Margarine was only for those who didn't care enough about the health of their families to buy butter. She was scornful of those who shopped at 'cut price' shops, believing strongly that we get what we pay for and that we should support the Co-op, even if it was more expensive. That is something of my mother that I still carry with me.

It's interesting how many new nutritional theories there have been in the last seventy years or so. During the war we were aware that all kinds of treats such as bananas and chocolate were either in short supply or were not available at all. With hindsight, I think that we who were children during the war, especially if we lived in the country, probably had a better balanced diet than any other generation of the twentieth century.

The only major setback I suffered happened in May 1937. It was common for garden fires to be lit at Clough Dene to get rid of garden rubbish. These fires could smoulder for days or even weeks and some of us showed our courage or, maybe more accurately, our foolhardiness by standing on the mound of earth covering the fire, shouting, 'I'm the king of the castle'. Unfortunately, I did this once too often. The outside covering of the fire collapsed and I found myself standing in red-hot ash that quickly melted the rubber of one of my Wellington boots. By the time the boot had been removed, my right leg was severely burnt from my thigh to my foot. There was talk of skin grafts, but that technology was still fairly new at the time and my leg was allowed to heal itself gradually.

For some time, the district nurse came every day to change the dressings and that was very painful. I must have cried, because I remember my grandfather coming to see me one day before the nurse arrived and telling me about the Spartans. He admired the Spartans and the message I took from him that day was that to be a Spartan was to be brave. When he left, he said to me, 'I want you to be a little Spartan from now on'. So when the nurse arrived, I knew that I couldn't cry any more.

I have many childhood memories of the growth of fascism. Before I went to school, I was aware of the burning of the Reichstag and during the Spanish Civil War I was totally on the side of the republican government against Franco's rebels. I couldn't understand how politicians in Britain and France could argue for non-intervention in Spain when it was so clear to my grandfather and my father that Hitler and Mussolini were using Spain as a training ground for the wider war that my father and grandfather were sure was bound to come. One of the images from that time that made an enormous impact on me was a picture in the *News Chronicle* of the effects of the raid on Guernica by German warplanes. One response was to help my mother when she went out collecting money and tinned food on behalf of the International Brigade of volunteers who went to Spain to fight for the government against Franco and his fascist allies.

The frustration with the British government that was felt in our house at Clough Dene became even greater when in August 1938 Hitler was given a green light to take over Czechoslovakia. There was nothing but ridicule for the Prime Minister, Neville Chamberlain, when he returned from his famous (or infamous) meeting with Hitler in Munich waving his piece of paper and talking about 'peace in our time'.

With hindsight, maybe we were all just a little hard on Mr Chamberlain because there was certainly no clear consensus for preparing for war in the ranks of either the Conservative or the Labour party at that time. There were those in the Conservative ranks who were sympathetic to Hitler, seeing him as a possible antidote to the Bolsheviks of the Soviet Union, but there was also a strong pacifist faction in the Labour party, still dominated by the pointless horrors of the First World War. It required the most urgent threat to our very survival in May 1940 to persuade the country to turn to a man who had for years recognised the threat of Hitler, Winston Churchill.

CHAPTER 2

Growing up, war, grammar school, music and cricket

The notes I handle no better than many pianists.
But the pauses between the notes – ah, that is where the art resides.
Artur Schnabel *Chicago Daily News*, June 11, 1958

ON FRIDAY 1 SEPTEMBER 1939, Hitler's Nazi army invaded Poland accompanied by ferocious attacks from the air. The British Government under Prime Minister Neville Chamberlain issued an ultimatum to the German Government calling for the immediate withdrawal of German troops from Poland. On that morning, I was delivering eggs to customers of my grandparents at Burnopfield and I remember hearing air raid sirens for the first time when they were tested. Then, I heard the radio broadcast at 11 o'clock on the morning of Sunday 3 September by Mr Chamberlain. He announced that as no reply to the ultimatum had been received from the German Government, Britain was at war with Germany. The air raid warning sirens sounded a few minutes later and I and everyone else wondered what would happen and how it would end. I was both excited and a little frightened, although I didn't doubt for a second that we would win.

Immediately, there was talk of food shortages being likely and those who could afford to, like my Aunt Polly, went out and bought as much tinned food as they could find room to store. Her wardrobes were packed with food, mainly tins of meat like corned beef. Many of the rest of us, having less money, criticised them as immoral hoarders so one immediate effect of the war was, at least for a time, to create divisions between families and friends.

In September 1939, I was just starting a new school year in Standard 4 at Pickering Nook School. A large air raid shelter, big enough to take all the school pupils and staff was quickly built on waste ground next to the school. It soon became my job to unlock the shelter each morning and lock it each afternoon after school. We were all issued with gas masks and there were regular practice

22

exercises using tear-gas when everyone left the classrooms and trooped out to the air raid shelter wearing our gas masks. It all seemed fun at the time but we had little idea of the reality of war.

There were also campaigns to boost National Savings and I took it upon myself to collect savings each week from people in Clough Dene where we lived. Every Friday morning I took the money to Hobson Post Office where Mrs Cawthorne made sure that the sums added up. Most people saved sixpence or a shilling each week and when anyone's savings reached fifteen shillings (only seventy five pence in today's money, but at that time about a quarter of the average wage at Hobson), the money was converted into a National Savings Certificate. Some years later, we understood that each Certificate would be worth twenty shillings and sixpence.

Our local authority, Stanley Urban District Council, like most councils, supported the savings campaign. There was a Warship Week, in which people in the area tried to save enough to buy a corvette, and also a Battle of Britain Week when we raised £30,000 to buy a Spitfire. I remember a large indicator like a thermometer fixed to the wall of the Council Offices in Stanley and each day it showed the current total amount that had been raised towards the target.

On a hill at Mountsett, not far from our home at Clough Dene and less than a mile from school at Pickering Nook, a bunker was built from which members of the Observer Corps kept watch for German bombers. Aeroplanes fascinated all of us at school and we competed with each other in building our collections of models of RAF planes from the range of Dinky toys. As the members of the Observer Corps were civilians, security at Mountsett was not as tight as it might have been. As a result, I somehow became accepted as a regular visitor to the Observation Post. There were pictures on the walls to help identification of the various German aircraft like the Heinkel 111 and the Dornier 17, known at the time as the 'Flying Pencil'. The pictures showed the bombers from the front, from the side and from underneath and I quickly became able to recognise them easily.

It was possible to see clearly Tyneside and the Sunderland area at the mouth of the Wear from the Observer Post at Mountsett using the binoculars used by the Corps. During the Battle of Britain in the summer of 1940 I used to count the scores of barrage balloons that were supposed to deter the German pilots from low-level attacks on the great shipyards on the Tyne and the Wear. In fact, there were not many large-scale bomber raids on the north-east, perhaps because the region was near the limit of the range of the German bombers, although I do remember clouds of smoke over Clough Dene one night when a German bomb hit a sugar warehouse at Newcastle. There were RAF fighter stations at Ouston, near Newcastle and at Usworth near Sunderland and there was always something very comforting about seeing a flight of RAF Spitfires or Hurricanes overhead.

For much of the war, my father worked as a member of the Rescue Squad based nearby in the Jubilee Hall at Tantobie, part of the national Civil Defence system. All the members of the Rescue Service were from the building trade and their responsibility was to use their knowledge of construction to search for and rescue anyone trapped in a building destroyed or damaged by bombing. Fortunately, Tantobie was never the target of a German air raid, so life in the Rescue Depot was generally quiet, although one night, a bomb did fall at Tanfield, about a mile away, breaking windows in the village and at the hospital nearby.

There was a table-tennis table in the Rescue Depot and I became quite good by playing with my father and his colleagues on his shift. Phil was also a good billiards player and for my eleventh birthday, he bought me a second-hand half-size billiards table. It soon became a main focus of social activities at Clough Dene, attracting cousins and uncles and their friends. Whenever there was a family get-together, my father usually organised a billiards handicap. It was difficult for the adults to take seriously the billiards skill of a boy, so my father was able to give me a good handicap for some time until I began to win too frequently!

Looking back now, it's interesting that family and friends all assumed that playing billiards was entirely a male pastime. On the other hand, when the billiards table became a table-tennis table by fitting the dining-table top, it was just as clearly assumed that my cousin Hilda and other girls would play. It's strange that to this day, although I've often seen good women table-tennis players, I can't remember seeing a woman top-class billiards or snooker player. Is that because of genes or environment?

By the time the war ended in 1945, my father had become Storekeeper at the Home Guard Depot in the Drill Hall in Stanley and I remember him taking me to a boxing tournament there. On VE night at the end of the war in Europe, there were many celebratory bonfires, but we were the only family with fireworks. I think that my father decided that as the war was over, the Home Guard wouldn't miss one box of thunder flashes!

My mother also played her part in helping the war effort by taking training courses in first aid and home nursing to qualify her to work voluntarily at the First Aid Post at Tanfield Lea School. She used to practise on me by putting my arm or my leg in splints. Often, her work involved night shifts and I remember saying goodbye to my mother as she caught a bus from Clough Dene to Tanfield Lea at about half past nine in the evening, to return at breakfast time the next morning. Sometimes my father and I would sit at his bedroom window watching the searchlights and the flashes of anti-aircraft gunfire around Sunderland, about fifteen miles away. On one occasion, I remember seeing an aircraft caught in the cross-beams of several searchlights for half a minute or so and then exploding as it was hit by the anti-aircraft gunfire. Seeing the multiple pieces of the German bomber glittering as they fell through the searchlight beams and knowing that I'd just seen several people killed is something that is still vivid in my memory, although I also remember thinking at the time that that was one less German bomber that might drop bombs on us.

The support of the family for left wing causes included uncritical admiration of the Soviet Union. As we saw it, Communists ran the USSR; Communists were on the side of the workers in their eternal battle against the forces of capitalism and so any criticism of the USSR in the capitalist press should be ignored. So we didn't believe the stories of purges in the USSR and even when the USSR signed a treaty with Hitler, we were still ready to understand and make excuses for Stalin.

Soon after the outbreak of war between Britain and Germany, the USSR invaded Finland. The Durham Miners Association decided to send a donation from union funds of, I think, £1,000 to Finland. My grandfather and his friend Harry Bolton from Chopwell (known, my father told me, from the days of the General Strike when miners at Chopwell were the last to abandon the strike as 'Little Moscow'), campaigned against this and were eventually expelled from the union. As he was an employee of the union, this created a very difficult situation for my grandfather. He and Harry Bolton brought a case against the union that was heard at Newcastle in 1941. A Newcastle solicitor named McKeag, then a prominent man in Newcastle United Football Club, represented John Jeffery and Harry Bolton. The case attracted some publicity in the national press and when they won their case against the union, I wasn't sure whether or not I welcomed the publicity.

On 22 June 1941 when Hitler sent his armies into the USSR, I remember waiting to hear the radio broadcast that night by the Prime Minister, Winston Churchill. From talking to my grandfather, I was a little afraid that Mr Churchill would announce that Britain was to join with Germany in a war to destroy communism, so my relief was total when the Prime Minister made a passionate speech welcoming the Soviet Union as an ally in the fight against Nazism!

Then on 7 December 1941, without a declaration of war, there was a devastating air attack by the Japanese on the United States fleet at anchor in Pearl Harbour. As a result, the enormous resources of the United States were added to those of Britain and the USSR in a powerful alliance against Germany, Italy and Japan in what was now truly a world war. For many of us still at school, the war had become an extended geography lesson. I had a *News Chronicle* map of the world pinned to our living-room wall and every night after the news on the radio, I moved the flags that marked the positions of the various armies.

By the autumn of 1941, I had moved from junior school at Pickering Nook to the Alderman Wood School near Stanley. At first, the war was a seemingly endless story of retreat in France, Holland and Belgium, Norway and Libya. Now the pattern was being repeated in the Far East. The only exception was the victory of the Royal Air Force over the Luftwaffe in the Battle of Britain in the summer of 1940, just after the evacuation of the British Expeditionary Force from Dunkirk. There were temporary victories under General Wavell over the Italians in Libya but they turned quickly into defeat when Rommel and his Afrika Korps entered the scene. At that stage, the Japanese and the Germans seemed almost invincible, but in spite of that I don't remember ever having any real doubt that eventually we would win and gradually, signs of better times ahead began to be seen. In October 1942, the British Eighth Army under Bernard Montgomery defeated Rommel's Afrika Korps at El Alamein in the Western Desert and soon afterwards the American army landed successfully in North Africa.

At about the same time, the siege of Stalingrad was lifted by Russian troops and in the process a vast German army was destroyed. These were major turning points and were followed by the successful British and American landings in Italy in 1943 and in France in 1944. Although we were all aware that many more battles lay ahead, these victories removed any uncertainty that any of us had about the eventual defeat of the German armies in Europe and of the Japanese in the Far East.

Most of my friends travelled to and from school on school buses but I usually cycled because there wasn't a school bus from Clough Dene, so I went home for my midday meal – always referred to by us at the time as 'dinner'. After the one o'clock news on the radio on 6 June 1944, I was able to hurry back to school with news of the first eye-witness reports of the Normandy landings by Allied troops. On D-Day in 1944, we all felt that it was now just a matter of time before the war was won. The realisation that it was possible to see an end to the war through the successes of the Allied Forces everywhere was a source of tremendous pride and satisfaction to a teenage grammar school boy accustomed to a set of beliefs that sometimes created a feeling of being marginalized. At last, I was able to feel that I belonged fully to the world of my school friends.

In August 1945, while I was on holiday with my maternal grandmother in Kenton in Middlesex, I went to Lords Cricket Ground to see one of the Victory Test Matches between England and the Australian Services Team that included great cricketers such as Keith Miller and Lindsay Hasset. At the end of the day's play on 8 August, I bought an evening paper and saw the first picture of the mushroom cloud over Hiroshima following the explosion of the first atomic bomb. Although I didn't question the decision to drop the atomic bomb, I understood that something truly dramatic had happened and that the world could never be the same again. The end of the war against Japan following the dropping of atomic bombs on Hiroshima and Nagasaki left all of us with feelings of relief that the war was at last over. I can't remember any doubts being expressed about the morality of the use of such a weapon at the time. After all, we knew that the Japanese had demonstrated little awareness of morality as we understood it, or indeed of the Geneva Convention, in their treatment of the prisoners of war that they had captured. By and large, we were just glad that, at last, the war was over.

The war years were a time when it began to be respectable to like jazz. As in every part of the twentieth century, there was a thriving popular music industry in the thirties. In the USA and in Britain, Bing Crosby was a hugely successful crooner and there were big bands such as Glenn Miller in the US and many dance bands in Britain, all very popular. I'm not sure how, but by the start of the war, I had begun to be excited by some of the less commercial American bands. Somehow, I'd begun to hear records of Louis Armstrong, The Original Dixieland Jazz Band, Duke Ellington, Coleman Hawkins, Benny Goodman, Artie Shaw, Woody Herman, the Nat King Cole Trio and many others. I wasn't particularly discriminating. When I listened to big bands, the faster and louder the music was, the more I liked it, but I did recognise that much of the music that the friends of my mother and father called jazz wasn't really jazz at all, but commercial popular music.

My mother once took me to tea with a friend in Tantobie who had just bought a new radiogram. She was very proud of it and said, 'Billy Cotton's jazz band is on the radio. Would you like to hear it?' My mother said, 'Oh, yes please' and I had great difficulty in hiding my childish scorn of such adult ignorance of what constituted jazz. Only quite recently have I heard a record made by the Billy Cotton band in the thirties that showed that it was a band that could play good jazz when it wasn't aiming at the commercial market so maybe my mother and her friend weren't as ignorant as I thought. My parents indulged my love of jazz but most of the teachers at school were scathing about what they tended to refer to as 'that noise'.

After the United States entered the war at the end of 1941, a big change came about. The BBC began to feature more American popular music, big band swing and jazz and the process of acceptance of jazz as a genuine musical form began. Gene Lees has accurately described the time as 'an era when a lot of popular music was good and a lot of good music was popular'. Within a few years after the war, American jazz musicians began to appear in the UK, although there were restrictions imposed by the British Musicians Union.

In 1948, I was able to hear Duke Ellington play piano with Ray Nance on trumpet and violin and Kay Davis singing, supported by the British musicians, the Jack Fallon Trio, at Newcastle City Hall. I also heard the great jazz pianist, Teddy Wilson, play there, and immediately after the war, many of us at school began to listen to short wave radio broadcasts from the American Forces Network in Europe, always referred to simply as AFN.

There were two similar AFN programmes that were the source of much argument among our 'hip' group at school. One was 'Midnight in Frankfurt' and the other was 'Midnight in Munich'. The style of both presenters was totally different from the formality of the BBC to which we were accustomed and I still remember the shiver of excitement when, after the midnight time signal, I heard 'Muffit' Moffat say, 'Twenty-four hours Central European time and it's Midnight in Munich', followed immediately by the Charlie Barnett band playing 'Skyliner'. Or there was Midnight in Frankfurt, with the signature tune 'Opus One' by the Tommy Dorsey band.

These programmes introduced me to the developing modern jazz of Dizzy Gillespie and Charlie Parker. At first, it was known as 'rebop', then 'bebop' later shortened to 'bop', and then back to 'bebop'. It was exciting and musically challenging and I suppose that those of us who liked it were somewhat inclined to write off as unmusical those who didn't. That was true whether those unconverted to bop professed to like classical music or New Orleans style jazz. In the late forties there was an enormous gulf between those who liked New Orleans or Chicago style jazz and those who liked bop and most members of either group were unable to hear anything worthwhile in the music of the others.

For reasons that I can't recall, we sometimes referred to those who liked New Orleans music as 'mouldy figs'. And when I raved about the Charlie Parker recording of 'Stupendous', a tune based on the chord sequence of George Gershwin's song 'S'Wonderful', admirers of the Benny Goodman version of 'S'Wonderful' were aghast. By 1949, Miles Davis had started yet another development in jazz when he recorded one of the all-time classic jazz albums *The Birth of the Cool*. Among lovers of modern jazz, 'cool' meant 'hip' or 'with it'. That was fifty years before the word 'cool' was adopted, in a slightly more general sense, as a new 'in-word' among another generation of teenagers (and quite a few aging swingers).

Earlier, in the late thirties and early forties, I had begun to enjoy classical music. I used to mark the details of classical music broadcasts listed in the *Radio Times*, especially if the programme included a

Rossini overture. At the age of eleven, my mother and my Aunt Dora took me to a matinée performance of *La Bohème* by the Carl Rosa Opera at the Theatre Royal at Newcastle. I didn't enjoy it much. The sets were dark and Mimi was so large that I couldn't believe that she was dying of consumption. But I continued to listen to overtures by composers like Rossini and Mozart on the radio and my father had records of Enrico Caruso singing 'La donna è mobile' and Lawrence Tibbett singing the 'Largo al factotum' among many others. One of these was and still is my favourite recording. It was issued on a ten-inch HMV seventy-eight rpm record and consisted of two wonderful duets by Amelita Galli-Curci and Tito Schipa.

Then, when I was thirteen, I went to the Theatre Royal with two fifth form girls from school. We saw Mozart's *Cosi fan Tutte* and I loved it. The sets were light, the atmosphere was wonderful and the whole experience was a joy. Perhaps the company of two attractive girls also helped!

When I left Pickering Nook School in 1941 and went to the Alderman Wood Secondary School at Stanley, the process was described as having 'passed the scholarship'. It took the form of an intelligence test that included such things as deciphering a simple code. I don't remember the test being described at that time as the 'eleven-plus', as it later became known. Pickering Nook was on the boundary of the catchments of Alderman Wood School and Hooker-gate School, near Rowlands Gill. As only Ernie Yard and myself from Pickering Nook passed the examination, and Ernie went to Hooker-gate, we both had to make a completely new start.

At first, it was difficult for me. Most of the boys and girls (all local authority secondary schools in County Durham then were co-educational) had many friends, having come as part of a group from Stanley, Annfield Plain, Craghead or South Moor, but I didn't know anyone. There was a little bullying of 'first years' by second-year boys, including being thrown over the school wall into a bed of nettles but few, if any, of us seemed really to suffer and most of us soon worked out how to defend ourselves.

Sport was one of the things that helped me to settle at the new school and I began to become more seriously interested in music. There were four houses, Dunelm, Neville, Watling and Tanfield (also the original name of the school, and the name by which it has again become known since becoming a comprehensive school). I was put in Neville house and began to play house junior cricket and football. I was also put in the top form in my first year. Alderman Wood was a good school. I was very proud of my new school blazer and I don't think it occurred to any of us to question the principle or system of selection. Probably that was because we'd been selected.

However, it seems to me that few human activities have been changed so often in the last fifty years as our educational systems, usually without any of the evidence that rational people would normally seek before making a decision. Politicians and educational-ists across the whole spectrum of opinion seem to me to make changes entirely on the basis of the current fashionable opinion within their sector. Then quite frequently, the new system is changed before enough time has elapsed to allow any proper evidence-based assessment. What's worse, there is little informed public debate about the purpose of education. As a result, although enormous sums of money are spent on education, there are almost as many ways of interpreting the outcome as there are educational commentators.

Gradually, I began to make friends at Stanley and some of them remained friends for life. People like Albert (always known as Bart) Hunter and Mary Martin who began going out together when we were all in the fourth year. Both became teachers before becoming husband and wife, Bart going on to become Headmaster of a secondary school at Chester-le-Street.

When I heard that I was going to Alderman Wood School (I think it was in April 1941), my father took me to Stanley and bought me a BSA bicycle on hire purchase from Dunn's in Stanley Market. I was tremendously excited and began to cycle a lot. In the summer of 1941, my cousin Ron took me and his brother Harry on a bike ride one Sunday. Ron intended that we should ride from Clough Dene to Hexham, from there, across the moors to Blanchland, back to Consett and home. It should have been a reasonably demanding ride of maybe fifty miles but that wasn't how it turned out. The road signs everywhere had been taken down in case of an invasion and we missed the Blanchland turning in Hexham.

For hour after hour, we pushed our bikes up steep hills and then rushed down the other side. Every time we approached the top of a hill, we hoped that we'd see the Consett Iron Company slagheap ahead, but each time we were disappointed by the view of another valley with another hill beyond it. Eventually, we asked someone if we were anywhere near Blanchland or Consett. He replied, 'I don't know about that, but St John's Chapel is at the bottom of this hill.' I'd never heard of the place, but Ron knew that it was upstream of Stanhope in Weardale and we were a long way from home. Fortunately, it was a fast road to Stanhope, but then we had to push our bikes for about three miles up Crawleyside bank on the road towards Consett. Ron pushed two bikes all the way, while my younger cousin Harry and I shared pushing the third bike. From the top, it was downhill almost all the way to Castleside, Consett and Clough Dene, and eventually we arrived home very tired after a truly memorable and exhausting day.

I joined the Youth Hostels Association and for several years, did quite a lot of touring on my bike. The two longest trips were in 1946. At Easter, my cousin Alan Rix and I cycled to York and after a night at the hostel there, we crossed the Pennines and stayed at a hostel near Glossop. From there, we climbed the Snake Pass in the Peak District and then passed Ladybower Reservoir on our way to stay with Aunt Lily at Belper, near Derby. After a few days there, we crossed into Lincolnshire and rode north to New Holland, where we took the ferry across the Humber to Hull. From Hull, we had to hurry to reach York in time for the evening meal at 7.30 pm and just made it in spite of a puncture. Then we cycled home the next day.

My second long tour was after the School Certificate exams later on in the summer of 1946. This time, I went with Edgell Parnaby, who went on to university to read, I think, physics. Edgell was a good friend who was the scorer for the school cricket team. Again, we went to York on the first day. Then we had a shorter trip to Tickhill, near Doncaster, followed by a leg to Grantham, another to Cambridge and thence to my Aunt Grace at Kenton for a few days. From Kenton, we cycled to Oxford and on to Stratford-upon-Avon. We saw *Macbeth* at the Shakespeare Theatre there before heading on to a hostel near Shrewsbury. Edgell and I then cycled across central Wales and stayed at Harlech Youth Hostel. Then we climbed over Snowdonia to a hostel on the North Wales coast and from there we rode to a hostel by Rudyard Lake, near Macclesfield. From Rudyard Lake, we crossed the Pennines to a hostel near Barnsley, continued back to York Youth Hostel and then home after a real adventure spread over three weeks and almost nine hundred miles.

I began to learn to play the piano at the age of eleven and was taught by a remarkable man in Burnopfield, a nearby village. His name was Arthur Blackburn and he having been brought up on a small Dutch island in the West Indies, his house was named 'Aruba House' after that island. It was a strange feeling to visit Aruba over 60 years later with my wife in 2005, when it was a port of call on a jazz cruise we took in the Caribbean. Mr Blackburn, as I always knew him, was paralysed down the whole of his left side and was always in a wheelchair. He had a powerful right hand and was perfectly capable of illustrating a musical point. I remember him introducing me with his one hand to the second movement, the allegretto, of the seventh symphony of Beethoven. To this day, whenever I hear that particular work, I am still reminded of Arthur Blackburn.

He was also a spiritualist and took *Psychic News* every week. He would read pieces to me 'proving' psychic phenomena in, I suppose, an attempt to convert me. In particular, he used to quote the famous scientists, Oliver Lodge and J J Thomson, in support of his spiritualist beliefs, and this was a strange experience for a twelve-year-old atheist who had assumed until then that scientists and the supernatural were always incompatible. I had first to try to consider whether the somewhat mystical scientific ideas of Lodge and others about the 'ether' (the medium through which it had been thought that radio waves were transmitted), and spiritualism might be right. Having rejected spiritualism, I asked myself whether the concept of the ether might be valid and decided that that was too vague to have any definable meaning.

Arthur Blackburn always listened to my arguments and never patronised me although I'm sure that I was a rather opinionated twelve- or thirteen-year old. Because I admired him, I had to work out ways of expressing doubt without giving offence to a man for whom I had enormous respect and for whom I felt real affection. It was good experience and a valuable demonstration to me that one could have mutual respect without necessarily agreeing about everything.

In my first year or two at Alderman Wood, the school did not have a specialist music teacher but in about 1943, JPB (Jack Percy Baker) Dobbs joined the staff. He was an inspiring teacher with an unusual ability to communicate his musical enthusiasm. The school set up a music society and I immediately became a member. Jack Dobbs organised group tickets for the seasons of concerts by the Hallé

Orchestra held at Newcastle City Hall each year in those days. About thirty members of the Music Society used to go by bus to Newcastle for the concerts that were held on Sunday afternoons. Our seats were on benches on the platform behind the orchestra. They were not very comfortable but they gave a wonderful view of John Barbirolli, the great conductor of the Hallé and they were cheap. One of my earliest memories of those concerts is of a dramatic performance of the fourth symphony of Tchaikovsky, but each was a major event to be looked forward to with keen anticipation.

I began to buy records whenever I could afford to and when Mr Dobbs suggested that some of us might add music to the list of subjects that we planned to take in our School Certificate examinations in 1946, I was one of those who agreed. Another was Margaret Dobson, who later married Bill Wilson who played cricket with me in the school team. Margaret went on to attend the Royal College of Music and sang for a number of years with the D'Oyley Carte Opera Company.

There was almost no flexibility in school timetables in those days so all of our music lessons had to be taken after normal school hours. That meant all of us, including Jack Dobbs, staying behind on three afternoons each week, but Jack Dobbs was such a good and committed teacher that none of us even considered dropping out. One of our set works was Mozart's Symphony No 40 in G minor, K550 and I still know just about every note of that wonderful work. I recall buying a recording of the symphony conducted by Toscanini at Windows music shop in Newcastle. It was on three twelve-inch 78 rpm records that cost nine shillings and eleven pence each. That was a major investment for me at that time! After our School Certificate exam, Jack Dobbs moved on from Stanley to become County Music Organiser for County Durham. He later became part of the academic staff at London University, before taking a post at Dartington Hall in Devon.

My recollection is that in order to pass School Certificate in those days, it was necessary to pass in five subjects and that there were three pass categories: 'pass', 'credit' and 'very good' (or maybe that was called 'distinction'). I passed my School Certificate in nine subjects, including music, with top grades in chemistry and geography, and credits in another seven subjects. I failed French but managed to achieve a pass the following year while working for my Higher

School Certificate. In 1948, I passed that examination in chemistry, physics, pure maths and applied maths, somewhat to the surprise of one or two of the teachers. One of them told me in my final year that I really must make up my mind whether I was going to be a professional cricketer, a professional musician or pass my Higher School Certificate. I seem to remember replying that I couldn't see why I shouldn't do all three – but maybe that's just what later I wished that I'd said!

Alongside that kind of assessment was the fact that when the senior chemistry master retired in 1946, he gave me his inorganic chemistry text book that he had used as an undergraduate at Birmingham University in 1903. His name was Mr Gunns (always known to the pupils as 'Bart' for reasons I never did discover), and he was a remarkable man with a powerful personality. Physical violence by teachers to pupils was still common in the forties, but Mr Gunns never struck anyone. Nevertheless, we were all terrified of his disapproval, so it was a great honour to be one of those singled out by him to receive one of his books, and I have it still.

I was fascinated by atomic theory and read a great deal outside the school curriculum. At the age of sixteen or seventeen, I borrowed from the school library a copy of a monograph by Erwin Schroedinger on wave mechanics. I struggled to make any real sense of it but I understood enough to know that here was something special. There was also at that time a publication by Penguin Books called *Science News* that came out, I think, quarterly. I bought it regularly and I remember being introduced to the idea of the newly-discovered particle, the meson, in one of those editions. The Atomic Energy Authority had been set up by then and I have a vivid memory of going to Newcastle Central Station to see the exhibition in what we referred to as 'the atomic train'.

That was my introduction to the demonstration of radioactivity using a Geiger counter. Most of us at Alderman Wood School at that time were stimulated by the possibilities of atomic power. We were excited by the prospect of treating cancers with radioactivity. We also saw atomic power as part of the way in which science could improve the lives of people around the world by providing energy that would not require men to descend underground every day to dig the coal that our society had needed since the start of the industrial revolution. Pesticides such as DDT were seen in a similar way at that time as a means of science helping the people of the world by producing more crops to feed the starving.

Nuclear power and some chemicals, including pesticides and products like thalidomide developed by the pharmaceutical industry, have sometimes turned out to have unforeseen and occasionally tragic consequences. No one would wish to play down the scale of a tragedy such as thalidomide but I do think that reactions generally are often based on demands for zero risk while tending to ignore benefits. Individuals take enormous risks with their own well-being, most notably through smoking cigarettes, over-eating, drinking too much alcohol and driving cars, but our society seems to expect zero risk when 'they', ie other people, are responsible. Another aspect of this is that generally speaking, our society (politicians, the media, men and women in pubs and their workplaces) treats every problem as a single issue, rather than considering how it links to and influences other problems.

Alongside my fascination with science lay my parallel interest in music and literature. Music I have mentioned, but the war years seemed to stimulate interest in the theatre and literature. At the end of the war, parties of pupils from school at Stanley began to attend performances of a wide range of plays at the People's Theatre in Rye Hill, near Scotswood Road in a run-down area of Newcastle.

I also became interested in the poetry of T S Eliot and remember buying a copy of 'The Waste Land'. It would be wrong to say that I liked it, but somehow it made a deep impression on me at the time and I still find it moving and somewhat disturbing. My father had a leather-bound copy of the complete works of William Shakespeare and I read the sonnets and most of the plays. After Higher School Certificate, I borrowed the complete plays of George Bernard Shaw from the branch of the County Library at Stanley and read them all before going off to join the RAF. And I loved the atmospheric writing of Raymond Chandler, even when (as often happened) I still wasn't sure of the identity of the murderer after finishing one of his books.

I also began an interest in quotations that has lasted all my life. Finding the lines:

> Thou hast committed –
> Fornication? But that was in another country, and besides, the
> wench is dead.

from *The Jew of Malta* by Christopher Marlowe was a special day for a teenage boy, even though the quotation didn't really make me want to know more about the Jew of Malta. One quotation that did make me want to read more of the work of the author was Mark Twain's, 'Water taken in moderation cannot hurt anybody' and I loved Tom Sawyer and Hucklebury Finn. Much later, 'A foolish consistency is the hobgoblin of little minds' introduced me to the essays of Ralph Waldo Emerson, via a scene featuring Barbara Streisand in the film *What's up, Doc?*

The period immediately after 1944 was a time of rapid changes in education. In 1944, the Minister for Education in the National Government was Mr R A Butler, known to everyone as 'Rab', and was the acceptable face of Conservatism in areas like County Durham, largely dominated by the Labour Party. He was responsible for the 1944 Education Act that changed the aspirations of so many of my and subsequent generations. Under the Act, instead of having to be sufficiently academically outstanding to win competitively a State Scholarship or a County Exhibition (as my cousin Ron had done in 1939), anyone passing Higher School Certificate and being offered a place at university would receive a County Exhibition automatically.

In 1950, the proportion of students going to university was, I think, still only about 2 per cent but the removal of the financial constraints that had in the past prevented so many talented people from considering university eventually changed the way generations of young people looked at the world. Many years later, when I was having dinner with Sir John Page, then Conservative Member of Parliament for Harrow West, a colleague and good friend (of whom more later), he asked me what I thought was the most important piece of legislation in my lifetime. Without hesitation, I replied, 'the 1944 Education Act'. He was a little surprised. Perhaps his own background of Harrow and Cambridge, plus the fact that in 1944 he had been serving with the British Army in Normandy, meant that the Act had had less significance for him than for me.

One minor result of the Act was the dropping of the name of 'Alderman Wood' from the school name. The school had been founded in 1912 as Tanfield School. It was originally designed to prepare young people for teacher training college. My mother was a pupil there for three years from 1916 to 1919 when she had to leave at the age of fourteen because her parents needed her to begin work. That was one of the very few things in her life about which my mother felt bitterness, even in her last years. She had really loved her three years at Tanfield School. Later, it became Alderman Wood Secondary School, and after the 1944 Act, for a period of perhaps a year, I think, the school became Alderman Wood Secondary Grammar School. This was soon changed to Stanley Grammar School. Years later, after County Durham adopted the comprehensive system, the school changed its name again and became Tanfield Comprehensive. *Plus ça change!*

The first four of the seven years I spent at Alderman Wood/Stanley Grammar School from 1941 to 1948 were dominated by the war, its horrors and its triumphs but at school, I was generally happy. I didn't much like many of the lessons apart from music and chemistry, but as I overcame my initial shyness, I made many friends. On most days, after our midday meal, the time before classes were resumed was spent by the boys talking or playing football with a piece of wood in the school yard, while the girls paraded back and forth along the terrace. On wet days, the boys were sent straight to their classrooms but the girls were allowed to dance in the School Hall and I began to be asked to play the piano for their dancing. At first, it was Scottish country dancing, but gradually we changed to a different kind of music, from Kern and Gershwin to 'Cow Cow Boogie'. I'm not sure that there was much dancing on those occasions, but some of the girls were appreciative and I enjoyed their attention.

Much later, in the summer of 1948 when I became captain of the school cricket team, I used to press-gang the junior boys on my dinner table to help roll the wicket before returning to their classrooms. I guess that I would have been in trouble with their parents if I'd done that fifty years later.

Stanley Grammar School had a good sporting reputation in the forties and several pupils became outstanding sportsmen nationally. Three especially come to mind, John Maughan, Ken Harrison and Bert Steward. John Maughan was the centre half of the school football team and after Higher School Certificate he went on to Oxford, where he got a blue. He was also a key player in the joint Oxford and Cambridge football team that called itself 'Pegasus' and won the FA Amateur Cup in 1951. John subsequently entered the Church of England, becoming a Canon.

Stanley Grammar School cricket team, 1948, author on extreme right

Another outstanding footballer was Ken Harrison who was the school centre forward. Ken had tremendous pace and a strong shot and once scored ten goals in a school match. Like John Maughan, he won an FA Amateur Cup medal when Crook Town beat Bishop Auckland after a second replay in 1954. In that same game, another friend, Jimmy McMillan, a former cricketing team-mate from a season in 1952 that I played for Kibblesworth, also won a cup-winners' medal. Ken Harrison also won English amateur international honours.

Finally, there was Bert Steward, an excellent cricketer as well as footballer. Bert also won an FA Amateur Cup medal and I played some cricket with him at school and at South Moor. But my main memory of Bert is of a comment he made to me at a school Harvest Camp in the summer of 1944. A large group of pupils with one or two masters, including Joe Binks, the art master at Stanley famous for his communist views, spent a few weeks at a farm at Trafford Hill between Darlington and Stockton. It was at that camp that Mr Binks made his classic remark that 'school would be all right if it weren't for the flipping kids'.

At fourteen-years old, I was the youngest member of the party and deemed to be too young to work on the farm so I was given the job of helping two fifth form girls, Dot Bell and Sheila Webb who were responsible with Mrs Clouston, the school cook, for feeding the party. Dot and Sheila were both good at hockey and tennis, something that added considerably to their attraction for a sport-mad adolescent and I had a very happy time peeling potatoes and such like while being looked after by the two glamorous girls. Just about every other boy at the camp envied me.

One day, Bert Steward said that he and some of the others were taking Dot and Sheila to a dance in the nearby village of Middleton One Row and invited me to join them. I'd never danced in my life, was still quite shy and was at a stage in my life when I thought that there was something a little iffy about dancing. Bert seemed to understand and he said, 'You play sport so you must have a decent sense of balance. That's a good start for dancing'. Suddenly, it seemed OK to go to a dance. I wonder whether I believed him. Probably, I just wanted to please him.

I was captain of the school cricket team in my final year and was very proud of that, especially on the day that we beat Bede College, Durham on the University ground at Durham. We managed to get them all out for about seventy-five and Bob Harrison (younger brother of footballer Ken) and I scored the runs required for a ten-wicket win. Many of us in that school cricket team played two games every Saturday, playing for the school in the morning and for local league clubs in the afternoon. Of the school team of 1948, our fast bowler, Brian Patterson, Norman Collin, Ernie Barras, Sid Lumley and myself all played for South Moor and there were many scrambles for buses to get from the school game on Saturday morning to the league game on Saturday afternoon.

I had played in 1947 for Tantobie, the club that my father had captained before the war and again in 1947 when the league resumed after the war. It was a good club then but played in a minor league, and when Billy Roxby, the captain of South Moor, the local Tyneside Senior League team, came to watch the school team early in 1948 and suggested that I join his club, I immediately agreed. My father had decided to retire from cricket because of ill-health at the end of the 1947 season and I felt sure that he would understand that I had to take the opportunity to play in a more challenging league. Looking back, I'm not sure that he did understand and I think that my father probably always felt a small hurt that I had rejected the club that had been such an important part of his life for many years before and immediately after the war.

South Moor had some outstanding local cricketers at that time. Men like Billy Roxby, himself a great leg spin bowler; George Storey, a tall, slim opening fast bowler who would bowl with great accuracy all afternoon if necessary and Billy (Chucky) Reynoldson, not built like an athlete but a tremendous square cutter of fast bowling. But the player that we all looked up to was Jackie Keeler, an opening batsman who certainly had the ability to have played first-class cricket regularly had Durham been a first-class county in those days. Keeler had played some good cricket in Australia while serving in the Navy during the war, gaining excellent experience and I remember him playing in his baggy Australian cap. I only played one season with him before he left South Moor to join Benwell in the Northumberland League as the club professional, but his skill, coaching and his general attitude to the game left a lasting impression on me.

Keeler's fielding at cover point was exceptional and he played three innings for Durham that I saw and that are worth recalling. In those days, Durham was one of the few minor counties regularly given a fixture against the touring team from overseas, and the matches were played at the Ashbrooke ground of Sunderland CC. At Ashbrooke in 1946, rain caused play to be abandoned, but in 1950, I went to see the West Indians when they came to Ashbrooke, and Keeler opened the batting for Durham. He just missed his century in each innings, scoring 91 and 97. Then, in 1952, he again opened the batting for Durham when the county played the Indians. This time, he made 135, reaching his hundred with a six, much to the joy of a huge crowd.

My years at Stanley Grammar School included the defeat of Germany and Italy in Europe and of Japan in the Far East. They also included the dropping of the first atomic bombs and the beginning of the Cold War, made clear to all of us by the blockade of Berlin by the USSR and the resulting Berlin airlift of 1948.

Many years later, in 1985 when I was attending a water conference in Tokyo with Dr Windle Taylor (a former Director of Water Examination at the Metropolitan Water Board that later became part of Thames Water), Windle and I flew to Hiroshima for a day. Even though, by that time, the city had been completely rebuilt, to see the spot above which the bomb exploded and see in the museum the consequences of the explosion of the bomb in August 1945 brought home to us the full horror of that day. In spite of that, I still feel that in the circumstances that existed in 1945, the decision to drop the first bomb was justified, although I am much less convinced by the logic of the decision to drop the second atomic bomb three days later on Nagasaki. What does need to be remembered is that had the war dragged on for another year or two, it is likely that many more people on both sides would have died.

CHAPTER 3

RAF, marriage, university and working for a living

Education is an admirable thing, but it is well to remember from time to time that nothing that is worth knowing can be taught

Oscar Wilde, *The Critic as Artist* (1891)

HAVING BECOME CONVINCED by one or two of my teachers that I was unlikely to pass my Higher School Certificate examination, I decided during my final year at Stanley Grammar School that I would give up any thoughts of university. Having no clear idea of what kind of career I hoped to have, yet realising that I had to make a choice of some kind, I decided that I would probably be offered a place at teacher training college. So I applied to Dudley Teacher Training College near Birmingham and was offered a place. In 1948, students going on to university straight from school were able to have their National Service deferred until after they had taken their degree but training college students were not deferred beyond the Higher School Certificate stage. So I left school for good in July 1948 and after two months of cricket, tennis and reading, I left home and my parents on Monday, 20 September to travel to RAF Padgate, near Warrington to join the Royal Air Force.

It was an experience that was simultaneously both exciting and a little frightening. It was little more than three years after the end of the war and memories of the Battle of Britain were still fresh in the minds of all of us, as was the glamour that had been associated with flying, fliers and the uniform. On the other hand, I'd been secure and sure of my place in my narrow society of family and school and was leaving behind all my friends to enter a world of which I knew nothing.

The eight days I spent at Padgate were mainly straightforward, being taken up with all the administrative details of documentation and issue of uniforms, but there was one difficult half hour. On the second or third day, we were lined up next to our beds in our billet and the Sergeant came in with a list of our names and began asking everyone to state their religion. I knew that it was legally possible to indicate that I had no religion but was uncertain of the practicalities and a little frightened. Slowly, the recruits down the side of the billet facing me answered Church of England or Presbyterian or Roman Catholic or whatever while I waited fairly fearfully for my turn to come. Eventually it did and when asked for my name and number I answered, '2405931, A/C Jeffery, Sergeant'. The Sergeant asked, 'Religion?' 'I don't have a religion, Sergeant'. 'Should I put you down as C of E then?' 'No, Sergeant, I'd rather you didn't'. 'Do you want me to put you down as atheist then?'

Much relieved that it had all been far more civilised than I'd feared, I replied, 'Yes, Sergeant'. When a day or two later, I received my identification disc, it had the letters 'ATH' underneath my name.

There was an interesting sequel to this episode. As soon as the Sergeant had left the billet, a row broke out in which most of the new young airmen were critical of religion. I found myself allied with the only two genuinely religious people in the billet, a Methodist and a Roman Catholic. The gist of our alliance was that we were the only people in the billet to have taken the question seriously. We argued that most of the others, not being religious, had simply taken the easy, but hypocritical, way out of allowing themselves to be described as C of E.

Having been kitted out at Padgate, we were ready for our general service training, otherwise known as 'square bashing'. There were, I think, four possible training camps and after much discussion of what we might expect, it was generally agreed that West Kirby was the camp to be avoided. So I was pleased to find that I was being posted to RAF Bridgnorth for my eight weeks' square bashing, despite it being further from home than the other primary training camps. On the morning of Tuesday 28 September, we marched through Warrington and boarded a special train to Bridgnorth. The doors were locked and somehow that made us begin to feel that we'd really joined up.

I hadn't looked forward to square bashing, but in fact, I enjoyed the experience. I found that I had a great deal in common with my fellow airmen, most of us having had our National Service deferred for a few months to allow us to complete our Higher School Certificate exams. It was interesting to find out how similar we were, whether we came from London, Lancashire, Lanark or County

Durham and it didn't take long to establish friendships. There were also a few surprises, such as the personal physical inspections known as 'FFIs' (free from infection) and the advice on contraception and prophylaxis given by the Medical Officer just before we were allowed to leave camp for the first time to go into Bridgnorth. I remember being amazed (and perhaps a little flattered) that the MO assumed that the first thing I was going to do on being let loose on Bridgnorth was to find a prostitute, and therefore, that it was vital that I understood the purpose of the Emergency Treatment (ET) room, situated immediately behind the Guard Room. I never did discover what devices or antiseptics were kept there.

At that stage of my life, although I'd had a number of girl friends, my sexual experience had been limited to cuddles in the back row of a cinema in Stanley. So on my first Sunday afternoon in Bridgnorth, I had a bit of a shock. The town was full of girls. Most of them had come in a fleet of coaches from Wolverhampton and were somewhat more forward than the girls from my sixth form at Stanley had been – as were the nurses who later came by coach from the local hospital to our station dances.

For four weeks at Bridgnorth, we learned to form up in threes, dress from the right, present arms, slope arms and obey the various other commands on the parade ground. I was reasonably fit from playing a lot of sport and enjoyed being physically tested. As a group, we began to take a pride in our performance and when we were given a weekend pass at the end of our first four weeks, I looked forward to going home and appearing at the Palais de Dance in Stanley in my RAF dress uniform. On my return to Bridgnorth, we began the second phase of our training. We were taught how to use a SMLE (short magazine Lee Enfield) rifle on the firing range and were trained on the assault course.

Eventually, the big day of our passing-out parade arrived, preceded by a special station parade to mark the birth of Prince Charles at which we all had to take off our hats and give three cheers. For weeks, we had been preparing for our passing-out parade with much ironing of uniforms and polishing of boots, using a candle to melt the boot polish to give a better shine. We passed out towards the end of November 1948 and were then given a pass to go home for seven days. It seemed like heaven to have a full week with nothing else to do but look up old friends and re-visit old haunts but it soon passed and I had to make the long train journey to No 2 Radio School, RAF Yatesbury, near Calne in Wiltshire to begin my training as a Ground Radar Assistant.

I did not enjoy the next few weeks anything like as much as I had enjoyed Bridgnorth. Yatesbury was miles from anywhere and it was impossible to travel home for a weekend although I did manage to enjoy a few weekends at Kenton in Middlesex with my Aunt Grace. The first part of the course consisted of electricity theory at a fairly basic level. Some of the civilian lecturers were not very good and one of the textbooks we used was just plain wrong. This was a training manual produced, as I recall, by the Admiralty in the twenties, so the section on atomic structure was more than a little out of date and I'm afraid I told the civilian instructor so. I should have found a kinder way but I suppose that I was just, as my father might have said, 'full of my own importance'. Perhaps we have to be hurt ourselves before we learn to stop to consider the feelings of others on such occasions.

Soon, we began to learn about radar and that was much more interesting. We learned about the introduction of Chain Home (CH) in the 1930s starting at Orfordness and RAF Bawdsey, near Felixstowe in Suffolk and the part that this had played in winning the Battle of Britain. CH was much more effective in detecting aircraft at high level than at low level and part of the success of the RAF in the Battle of Britain was due to a wrong assumption made by the Germans. We were told that they had heard something about an aircraft detection system being developed by Britain, but guessed that it would be most effective at low level and so made most of their early bombing attacks at high level, which was perfect for the energy distribution of the CH system. By the time the Luftwaffe began to consider that they might have made a wrong assumption, the RAF had access to Chain Home Low (CHL), a system with a shorter wavelength than CH and therefore able to detect aircraft effectively at lower altitudes. Soon after that, the very short wavelength (3,000 megacycles frequency, 10 cm wavelength) oscillators, the magnetron and the klystron became available, making possible the detection of aircraft at very low levels of a few hundred feet above the sea.

It was fascinating stuff and I looked forward to working with real equipment. However, when I finished my course at Yatesbury, RAF Records Office at Gloucester, in their infinite wisdom, posted me to RAF Medmenham between Marlow and Henley in Buckinghamshire. RAF Medmenham was the headquarters of 90 Group, which was the RAF signals group, so I suppose the posting must have made sense to someone at RAF Gloucester. But Medmenham was a purely administrative station, so no one knew what to do with an individual radar technician. I spent four weeks of my National Service sweeping up leaves while a new posting was sorted out with RAF Gloucester.

Apart from road sweeping, I managed to play a couple of games of football for the station team and made a few more visits to my Aunt Grace at Kenton. During one of those, I went to Wembley Town Hall to hear a concert by the London Philharmonic Orchestra conducted by the great Sir Thomas Beecham.

On another occasion, I was ordered to be a member of an escort party at the funeral of a young airman who had hanged himself in a lavatory at Medmenham. A military funeral was a completely new experience for me. We slow marched out of the camp behind the hearse and after a hundred yards or so, changed to quick march until just before we reached the church in the village of Medmenham, when we went back to slow march. After the funeral, we fired a volley of shots over the grave. Curiously, the tiny village of Medmenham was to become important to me starting fifteen or so years later as the site of the laboratory of the Water Research Association (now WRc plc), with which I was involved for many years.

Then, in early March 1949, I was posted to RAF Sutton Bridge, the headquarters of the Northern Signals Area of 90 Group near King's Lynn. Once again, I'd been sent to a station that had no radar, and I began to wonder whether it was a plot to reduce the risk that I might wreak havoc with the equipment. I spent a week there, mostly in an open hangar with the icy east wind from Siberia whistling through it, learning how to dismantle and assemble a Sten gun with frozen fingers.

From Sutton Bridge, I was eventually posted to RAF Dimlington, a small ground radar station near the village of Easington on Spurn Point in East Yorkshire, south of the small seaside resort of Withernsea. Dimlington was an isolated site with 10 cm wavelength radar gear and from time to time, in bad weather, we received a request from Filey coastguards to mount a shipping watch. These requests were not popular, because even if we did pick up a signal from a ship, it moved so slowly that there were long periods of inactivity. However, on one occasion when I was one of the small team on shipping watch, we received a series of increasingly anxious calls from Filey asking us to check whether there was any sign of a ship close to land. We kept on looking at the screen and not seeing anything that looked like a ship until finally, the coastguard rang again and said, 'You'd better have a walk outside and look over the cliff. The ship's now gone aground on the beach underneath you'. What had happened was that the ship had been within less than three miles of the shore when we were called out, and at that range, the 10 cm radar picked up such a strong signal from the waves – known as wave clutter – that the signal from the ship couldn't be distinguished from it. Fortunately, no one was hurt.

The summer of 1949 was warm and sunny and I had a wonderful time. I was made captain of the station cricket team and played cricket against many of the village teams in East Yorkshire as well as playing tennis and getting to know the girls of Withernsea.

At weekends, I usually left camp at about 6.00 a.m. on Saturday to catch the bus from Easington to Hull and then took the train from Hull to Newcastle, so that I could play cricket for South Moor in a league match in the afternoon. Then, on Sunday evening, I used to catch the last bus from Stanley to Durham to take a train from there to York.

The train to Hull left York at about half past three on the Monday morning, arriving in Hull before six o'clock for the half past six bus to Easington. There was a small café near the bus station and after a pint mug of scalding tea, I boarded the bus and after over an hour in the bus, arrived back at the guardroom just before the deadline of 08.00 hours, ready to go on duty after a wash and shave. It was a fairly hectic schedule but at the age of nineteen, it seemed perfectly normal to me at the time.

One of the features of the summer of 1949 was a strike in the London Docks and four of us were sent from Dimlington to RAF North Weald in Essex, a former Battle of Britain fighter station. We were part of a group of 104 airmen from Northern Signals Area, all sleeping under canvas. On the first morning we were there, we were told on parade that airmen were to be sent to London Docks to help unload a shipload of ball bearings. The four of us from RAF Dimlington promptly decided that there was nothing to be gained by being at the front of the queue. As we had surmised, either the managers at the docks or the RAF (or more likely, both) would think in round numbers and it turned out that 100 airmen were required. As we four were at the end of the queue, no one wanted us and we were given the day off.

I knew that there was a cricket match that day at Lords Cricket Ground between the Royal Air Force and the Royal Navy and it seemed to us that we had a duty to support our fellow airmen. So the four of us took the underground from North Weald to St John's Wood and had a wonderful day. We saw Peter May, playing for the Royal Navy, play one of the finest innings I've ever seen. That night, I wrote to my father telling him about Peter May. I said that I felt sure that he would play for England within two years and almost exactly two years later, May made his debut for England, scoring 138 against South Africa.

At the end of August 1949, I was posted to RAF Bawdsey, near Felixstowe in Suffolk. Bawdsey was famous, having been the first operational radar station in the world when it opened a couple of years before the war. The original CH equipment was still in use, as was the later version, CHL. I was assigned to the maintenance of the newer 10 cm wavelength equipment known as NT 277 (Naval Type 277), which was the same as I had become familiar with at RAF Dimlington. Once again, I was quickly involved in sport. I played regularly for the station football team and was also drafted in occasionally to play rugby and hockey for the station throughout the winter of 1949–50.

At about this time, I realised that most of my RAF colleagues with a similar Higher School Certificate background were planning to go to university after their Air Force service, and I began to reconsider my plans for teacher training college. Eventually, I applied for a place at King's College, Newcastle (then the Newcastle division of the University of Durham), to read chemistry. I was interviewed by Professors Clemo and Wynn-Jones and I remember being asked by Professor Wynn-Jones whether I'd kept up my studies while in the RAF and giving a somewhat evasive reply.

Wynn-Jones then said, 'I expect there were rather a lot of smoking concerts.' I'd no idea what he meant, but it sounded as though he was talking about an acceptable social activity so I was happy to agree. I was offered and accepted a place to join the first year honours chemistry course to begin in the autumn of 1950.

At the time, that seemed to be a long time away to a nineteen-year old rarely looking more than a week ahead. I didn't do any serious revision of my school science, although I read many books on science, books like Sir James Jeans' *The Growth of Physical Science*. I also kept up my interest in understanding the structure of the atom and the particles of which it is composed that had developed at school by reading about the work of people like the Curies and Becquerel, Einstein, Max Planck, Nils Bohr, Erwin Schrodinger, Heisenberg and others. I and many of my friends had been fascinated by these advances whilst at school. To us, they had not only made possible the horrifying destructive power of the atomic bomb (which had, nevertheless, brought about a rapid end to the war), but had also opened up the many possibilities of atomic energy. But overall, my life in the RAF was exciting and enjoyable, and there were too many things to do to be able to fit them all into the day so there was little time to worry about the next year or the challenges of science.

Bawdsey Manor where I served from August 1949 until April 1950 was an attractive country house overlooking the beach. I always understood that it had once belonged to the de Coverley family but more recently I've read that the Air Ministry bought the manor and land from the Quilter family. In 1949 part of the manor was the Officers' Mess, while the 'erks' such as we radar technicians used the rest of it as a place for sitting around chatting, and for occasional amateur dramatics and station dances. It was a tranquil place in those days, quite unlike other RAF stations on which I had served.

In that setting, in between the games, reading and work at RAF Bawdsey, I met a WAAF radar operator from South Wales called Mavis Carroll. She was eighteen years old and I was nineteen and in the summer of 1950, we were married. We both required parental consent to marry and I asked my parents if they would agree. They thought that we were both too young and they were also worried that marriage would lead me to give up the idea of going to university. They said that they would only give their consent to the marriage if I took up my place at university and that was agreed. In October 1950, I registered for the first time as a student at King's College, Newcastle.

There were several undergraduate fathers at King's College at that time, many of the second- and third-year students having served during the war and many were in their middle to late twenties. But in my first year group of 1950–51, only a few of us had completed our National Service, so it was a rare event for a first-year student to be married, let alone become a father. So when my first daughter, Wyn, was born, it brought me a certain amount of status among my peers.

The Chemistry Department at King's College was highly competitive in the early fifties. About forty-five of us began the first year of the Honours Chemistry course in October 1950 and following the end-of-year examinations in June 1951 about half were retained in the Honours School. I had found my return to full-time study difficult and didn't make the cut, but the rules at that time allowed me to transfer to a pass degree course. Physics had been one of my subsidiary subjects, along with botany. I had found parts of the physics course particularly difficult and decided that I had to find another subject to combine with chemistry in my second-year studies.

I discussed with my tutor what I might do and he suggested, 'Why don't you think about doing bugs?' 'What's bugs?' 'Bacteriology'. 'I suppose it can't be worse than physics'. 'OK, I'll fix a time for you to meet Professor Dunlop, who heads the department'.

Apart from my first-year undergraduate botany course I had no background in biology and had no idea what a bacterium was, beyond the admonitions from my mother in childhood to wash my hands to get rid of germs. But I went to see Professor Dunlop anyway. Within half an hour, he had fired my imagination and stimulated my interest in an academic subject in a way that no one else except my old music teacher, Jack Dobbs, had either at grammar school or at university, and I enrolled in the Bacteriology Department, beginning my second year at King's College studying chemistry, bacteriology and botany.

I was quickly much happier. I had always been interested in chemistry and I was lucky that the head of botany, Professor Thomas, was only really interested in plant physiology. As a result, I was able to get by without worrying too much about the classical botany of classification, morphology and such in which I had little interest. But my introduction to bacteriology was the real bonus. I found the subject fascinating and still do, and for the first time at university, I began to feel that I was valued. People like Muriel Emslie-Smith and her husband, both lecturing in the Department, began to make me feel that they thought it was worthwhile to give me their time and I began to sense that I was getting somewhere.

June 1953 was an amazing month. Sir Edmund Hilary and Sherpa Tensing succeeded in climbing Mount Everest after so many had failed; the Australians were playing a Test Series in England; there was the Coronation of Queen Elizabeth II and I took my final examinations for the degree of BSc. Having been kicked out of Honours Chemistry, I had found it hard to believe that I would obtain a degree, but two small events raised my hopes.

During several vacations, I had worked in a National Coal Board laboratory near Stanley, and at the end of my last stint there, Mr Muddiman, the Area Chief Scientist and a god-like person to us junior laboratory assistants, called at the laboratory. As he was leaving, he looked in to see me and said simply, 'If you want a job when you graduate, come and see me.'

Then, a few months later, towards the end of my bacteriology *viva*, Professor Dunlop asked me, 'What are going to do after you graduate?' My self-confidence had taken a severe knock in the summer of 1951 so these indications that two people that I respected took it for granted that I would graduate (there was a significant failure rate in those days) were a great boost to me.

On the last Friday in June 1953, our examination results were due to be posted on the college notice board. My friends and I arrived at King's College in the morning and seeing that the results had not been posted, we went off to nearby Exhibition Park in Newcastle to play tennis. When we returned, there was still no news and as the afternoon wore on, I realised that I was going to have to leave without seeing the results because I had to be in Stanley by quarter past five to play cricket in an evening cup tie. That was a real anticlimax and frustration. After the cricket match, I went home and at half past nine in the evening, my father said, 'Come on. If we catch the twenty-five to ten bus, we'll have time to walk up to the college, see the results and catch the last bus back to Stanley'.

We arrived at the notice-board at about half past ten, and to my delight, I saw my name on the list of those successful. My father and I set off back towards the bus station and after about a hundred yards, I asked my father to confirm that he had seen my name on the list. He replied, 'No, I didn't have my glasses on'. So I made him return with me to the notice-board, put on his glasses and confirm that, yes, my name was on the list. We then just managed to catch the last bus home from Newcastle. It was a truly wonderful feeling to know that the years of sacrifice, especially by my mother and father, had not been wasted and I could start to think about a future as some kind of scientist.

In December 1953, soon after my graduation, our second child, Carole, was born at the Richard Murray Hospital, at Blackhill, near Consett, County Durham. There were now six of us living in my parents' small three-bedroom house, but by that time, I had a job and was able to think about finding a place of our own, easing the family stresses. I realise now that the emotional cost to my mother and father of enabling me to take my degree was considerable, and I am much more grateful to them than I ever succeeded in expressing to them at the time.

As we were still living with my parents, I had to find work within daily travelling distance of Stanley and I remembered that I had been invited by the area Chief Scientist of the National Coal Board (NCB), to contact him. At an interview at his office at Shotley Bridge near Consett, Mr Muddiman offered me the post of Assistant Chief Chemist at Norwood Coke Works at Dunston, in Gateshead. I accepted and on Monday 27 July 1953, I began my first 'proper' job at a salary of £485 per year on a scale rising through fourteen annual increments of £30 to £805 per year at the top of the scale. It may not have been as exciting a prospect as I might have imagined, but I had a real job and with it, my first opportunity to prove to myself and to others that I had something to offer.

My father was fond of saying of almost any example of human frailty, 'Some people will do anything but work for their living', so I was glad that, at the age of twenty-three, I at last had a job and was able to look him in the eye.

My monthly salary was to be paid into my bank account so I had to open an account, something my father had never needed to do. Unfortunately, as I was paid monthly in arrears and had no money to deposit, I was not given a cheque book until the beginning of September, after my first pay cheque, covering five weeks' work, had been processed. That period seemed never-ending, but what a day it was when I was able to write my first cheque and draw some of my first proper salary.

Norwood Coke Works was a major plant in a poor part of Dunston in Gateshead, next to the rope works. It carbonised one thousand tons

Author's parents with their granddaughter Wyn

of coal each day, every day of the year, and discharged effluent into the small River Team that quickly entered the River Tyne. The works produced high quality foundry coke for use in steel manufacture, then still a massive industry in the region. The process included extraction of various by-products from the coal gas, itself a by-product of coke production. Some of the gas was used to heat the coke ovens and the remainder sold to the Gas Board for blending with the town's gas that it produced from different types of coal in various gas works.

We also extracted ammonia from the gas by forcing it through saturators containing sulphuric acid, producing ammonium sulphate for use as a fertiliser and recovered crude benzole from the gas by passing it through benzole scrubbers. The crude benzole was then distilled to produce fractions containing benzene, xylene and toluene. These products were sold to the National Benzole Company for blending in that company's petrol products.

There was also a tar works, operated by a company called Thomas Ness Ltd that was mainly owned by the NCB and which produced various tar products such as naphthalene from the residues of the coke works' by-products' recovery process. It was a smelly and dirty plant that would have horrified a health and safety inspector a couple of decades later, but it was an interesting works and the job gave me some excellent experience of how industry worked at that time.

There was a lot to learn and my new colleagues were very kind and patient with me. My practical knowledge was limited to what I had picked up about coal analysis during my vacation work experience. I started work knowing nothing of coke manufacture or of the routine gas and benzole analysis that was such an important part of the work of the laboratory. The patience of the laboratory staff allowed me gradually to begin to understand a little about the supervision and motivation of a small group of intelligent laboratory assistants, almost all studying at technical college through day release for Ordinary or Higher National Certificates in chemistry, and in a few cases, for membership of the (then) Royal Institute of Chemistry.

One day, Mr McGovern, the manager of the coke works, called me into his office. He said, 'I've had a visit from a River Board Inspector. He says he thinks that we've polluted the River Team and he gave me a sample that he's taken from the river. Can you tell me what the white deposit is?' He handed me the sample and I said, 'I'll see what I can do'.

I was quite pleased to receive such a challenge, but a little worried as qualitative inorganic analysis had never been one of my strengths at university. I put the sample through the standard procedures I had been taught. The only metal I could find was zinc and I could not detect any of the common acid radicals such as chloride or sulphate. This was very puzzling and I felt certain that I had done something really stupid. Mr McGovern had given me no hint of whether he had any idea of what the substance might be or where it might have originated, so I repeated the procedures. Again, I found only zinc. I did the tests a third time, by now somewhat desperate, and again found only zinc. The manager was waiting for me to tell him my results, so I went to his office to tell him that I'd failed.

I said, 'I'm sorry, but the only metal I can find is zinc and I can't find a single acid radical. That suggests that it might be zinc oxide, but as we don't have any zinc compounds here, I can't imagine that that could be right.' Mr McGovern laughed, and replied, 'I hoped it would turn out to be zinc oxide. That means that the pollution is probably coming from effluent from the chemical works at Birtley' (a few miles upstream of Norwood Coke Works on the River Team). That was my first ever involvement with a problem of water pollution.

Whilst at Norwood, I saw something that I sometimes quoted in later years when I became involved in the work of British Standards Institution on the design of sampling programmes. I was walking through the Coke Works alongside a train of wagons full of coal that was being delivered to the coal washery, to be blended after washing to give the right blend of quality for production of foundry coke. Bill, the coal sampler, was taking samples of coal from the tops of the wagons with a sack and a shovel before taking the composite sample to his workshop next to the laboratory for preparation for analysis by a process known as grinding and quartering. After he'd prepared the coal sample, it would be analysed in the laboratory for sulphur content, ash, volatile matter, etc.

As I walked towards him, I saw that from time to time Bill threw something over the side of the wagon onto the ground. When I reached him, I asked, 'What're you throwing away, Bill?' 'Oh, that's the stones. You don't want them, d'you?' So much for the accuracy of the laboratory results for ash etc!

For about eighteen months, I was happy at Norwood. I found the whole operation fascinating and liked my colleagues. With hindsight, it was a pretty unpleasant environment in which to work, surrounded as we were by carcinogenic chemicals, but none of us thought about the health risks, or much about healthy living generally at that time.

In those days, we worked a five and a half day week and on winter Saturdays, after the morning's work, those of us playing football for the Coke Works' team used to gather in the Eslington Arms, next to the Works. After a pie and a pint or two, I and the rest of the Coke Works' team played football in a local league, so I got to know a number of people that I didn't meet in the laboratory. I enjoyed playing football, but as showers were unheard of among the teams in that league and I didn't have a car, the games were followed by a long journey home by bus, almost always with muddy (and sometimes bloody) knees. That wasn't so pleasant.

A few unusual projects also came my way, such as the operation of a pilot plant to investigate the possible extraction of pyridine by steam distillation of the crude benzole produced as a by-product of coke production. This was another experience that would have been almost impossible under later health and safety legislation, given the various unpleasant physiological properties of pyridine.

Then early in 1955, I received a phone call at Norwood from Dr Hall, the Divisional Chief Scientist of Durham Division of the NCB. Dr Hall seemed like someone from another planet to those of us working in the laboratory at Norwood Coke Works. No one there had ever met him, so it was remarkable for an unknown young scientist to receive a phone call from the great man. He said that someone in personnel had mentioned that I had combined bacteriology with chemistry in my degree and that he would like to talk to me about an effluent treatment problem. Dr Hall had already been in touch with my manager, Mr McGovern, so a day or two later, I went to the NCB Durham Divisional Laboratory in Forth Lane, off Pink Lane in Newcastle to meet the Chief Scientist.

He told me that it was becoming increasingly important and difficult to meet the regulatory requirements for effluent discharges from coking plants set by the River Boards since the Rivers (Prevention of Pollution) Act had become law in 1951. The NCB was planning a new coke works at Fishburn in County Durham, and in order to get consent for the construction, the Board had been required to give an undertaking to build an effluent treatment plant to remove phenols, thiocyanates etc. A commercial ion exchange plant was going to be built as the only way of satisfying the River Board but it was going to be expensive to operate and the NCB was keen to investigate other options for other coke works.

Dr Hall said that a man called Forlin, working for the NCB in South Wales, was researching the use of bacteria to break down phenols and asked me to go to see Forlin and write a report on the possibilities. He said that he thought I would be away from Norwood for about three weeks. I travelled to South Wales early in February 1955 and when Dr Hall had read my report, he said that he wanted me to move immediately to his laboratory and begin an investigation into the biological removal of phenols etc, from Durham coal carbonisation effluents. I did not return to Norwood and began an eventful six-year period of research that changed my life.

The first stage of the research was to study published work on the subject and learn something of the micro-organisms capable of breaking down phenols and thiocyanates; also such things as their nutrient requirements and optimum temperature for growth, bearing in mind that this temperature might not be the same for breaking down thiocyanates as for phenols etc.

After a few weeks, I began operating a laboratory scale-activated sludge plant in the laboratory at Forth Lane in Newcastle. It required daily attention, so for some considerable time, I travelled by bus seven days a week from home to Newcastle to check on the progress of the experiment.

The response of the system to different conditions of temperature and rate of supply of air was fascinating and quickly became an absorbing interest. The Divisional Scientific laboratory was a good and stimulating place to work because of the people there and the varied range of problems being investigated. For example, my colleagues in the laboratory were working on a number of other important projects including research into the causes of pneumoconiosis and silicosis and effective methods of dust suppression in mining. As well as making a number of good friends, I felt that I was doing something really worthwhile for the state of our rivers many years before anyone thought of the term 'environmentalist'.

After a year or so, we had gathered enough basic information to design a large-scale pilot plant that was to be built at Lambton Coke Works, near Fence Houses in County Durham. There, I repeated the laboratory scale work and showed that the results were reproducible on the larger scale.

While I was working at Lambton, I was taught an important lesson about human behaviour. A minor adjustment to the pilot plant was required and I asked the foreman fitter if he would arrange for one of his fitters to do the work. He replied that any of the fitters could do what was needed and that I should just go to the fitting shop and ask one. But he added, 'Make sure that you ask someone who's busy and he'll find time to do it. If you ask someone doing nothing, he'll have a hundred reasons why he can't help you'. Over the years, I've seen countless examples of the general truth of that foreman's advice.

Many senior staff of the Coal Board visited Lambton Coke Works at that time to see the pilot plant and discuss with me the research programme on phenol removal. The man who impressed me most was Dr Jacob Bronowski, then head of the Coal Board research establishment at Stoke Orchard near Cheltenham and at that time, already a BBC personality. He arrived at Lambton one morning wearing one of his trade mark flamboyant kipper ties. Within an hour or so, by asking the right questions (and, unusually, listening to the answers), he showed that he understood what we were trying to do in a way that few other visitors came close to doing.

By about 1957, it was time to use the data from the pilot plant to design a full-scale effluent treatment plant to be built at Brancepeth Coke Works, near Willington in County Durham, where discharges of phenolic effluents had on several occasions killed young salmon in the River Wear near Page Bank, just north of Spennymoor. The plant operated successfully and in 1958, I was invited to give a paper describing the research to a meeting in Durham of the Coke Oven Managers Association, the professional body of managers, engineers and scientists in the coking industry. I had earlier been asked to contribute to a national conference on water pollution in Church House Westminster, but the meeting in Durham was different, because it was the first time that I had presented a full-scale paper as an individual. I remember how nervous I was, but everyone was very kind, the discussion went well and I went home feeling fairly pleased with myself. My career seemed to be developing in the right way.

CHAPTER 4

All change

We cannot remain consistent with the world
Save by growing inconsistent with our past selves

Havelock Ellis, Preface, *The Dance of Life* (1923)

SOON AFTER I BEGAN my research in 1955 on biological removal of
phenols from carbonisation effluents, I went to see Mr Miller, one
of my former lecturers in the bacteriology department at King's
College. I wanted help and I also wanted to explore the possibility of
submitting a thesis for a higher degree, perhaps for a PhD, seeing that
partly as a way of overcoming the disadvantage of having only being
awarded a pass degree. Although they were early days in the project,
I realised that an academic thesis might require information not
strictly necessary for the purposes of the NCB project. It quickly
became clear that the bacteriological content of the research was
highly unlikely to be sufficient to underpin a thesis likely to be
accepted by the bacteriology department, but Mr Miller suggested
that I contact Peter Isaac, who was in the process of creating a public
health engineering section within the Department of Civil Engineering at King's College, in Durham University.

I arranged a meeting with Peter Isaac. It emerged that in the
University of Durham at that time, it was not possible to take a PhD
through a thesis describing external work. That would have been
possible at the University of London, but only if one had a first
degree from London, so I had a slight feeling of frustration. On the
other hand, a thesis for a Master's degree describing external work
was possible and Peter Isaac was enthusiastic about my project as a
suitable subject for a thesis for a Master's degree in applied science.

Over the next three or four years, Peter Isaac and his colleague Bill
Simpson, who became my academic supervisor, were both very
supportive and early in 1960, I received a letter from the university
telling me that my thesis had been accepted for the degree of MSc.
In the summer a few months later, I received my degree in a
Congregation in the Great Hall of Durham Castle. It was a truly

60

memorable occasion for me and I was delighted that my mother was able to be there to share the occasion with me after all the sacrifices she had made.

In June 2002, there was a kind of sequel. I had met Peter Isaac from time to time over the intervening years, for example, when I gave evidence in the 1980s on behalf of the Water Companies Association to the House of Lords' Committee on Science and Technology and he was the Assessor appointed by the Committee. I knew that he had retired after having been Professor of Civil Engineering at the University of Newcastle upon Tyne because I saw him occasionally at university functions. One day, I received a letter from Peter telling me that he was a member of the Senior Common Room at University College, Durham and inviting me to be his guest at a dinner on 11 June in the Great Hall of Durham Castle. I collected him from his home at Wylam and had a thoroughly enjoyable evening.

On the way home, I mentioned that I had started work drafting on my computer some memories of my life. Peter said that he'd had a lot of experience in setting up papers and other documents on computer and immediately offered to help by formatting the work for me. He also asked, 'Would you be interested in becoming a member of the Senior Common Room at University College?' 'Yes, of course I would. It would be a great honour'. Peter replied, 'Well, you must realise that an invitation is entirely at the discretion of the Master, but I'll have a word with him'.

I dropped off Peter at his home and next day wrote to him to thank him for his hospitality. Then at the weekend, it was an enormous shock to receive a message from Mrs Isaac telling me that Peter had died. She said that my letter had arrived on 15 June but he had been too ill to read it and had died later that day. At the funeral a week later, Wylam church was packed and I was almost the last person to leave after the service. Mrs Isaac was remarkable. She had spoken to everyone as they left the church and when I reached her, although she hardly knew me, she said, 'I know that Peter wanted to put you forward for membership of the Senior Common Room, so I've spoken to the Master and he's expecting you to speak to him. He's standing over there. Do go and introduce yourself'.

I did so, and in October 2002, after having lunch with the Master, Maurice Tucker, I became a member of the Senior Common Room of University College, Durham. I cannot imagine many people thinking of doing what Mrs Isaac did for me in such sad circumstances.

In the 1950s, building societies normally required a deposit of 10% before offering a mortgage. For me, that was about £200 and with an annual salary of around £700 it was practically impossible to save £200 in a reasonable time. However, NCB rules allowed for the Board to make an advance on mortgage of 100% of the price of a house to a member of staff required to move to a new place of employment and I saw that this offered a way out.

I had transferred from Norwood Coke Works' staff to NCB Divisional Scientific Department in Newcastle, but by the spring of 1957, I was spending most of my working time running the pilot effluent treatment plant at Lambton Coke Works. I didn't have a car and I made the case that it would be more sensible for me to be based at Lambton Coke Works and live nearer Lambton. That would allow me to be more easily able to deal with any emergencies, rather than travelling by bus from home at Clough Dene to Newcastle and then by bus from Newcastle to Lambton. My proposal was accepted and as a result, I was able to borrow the full purchase price of £1,895 to buy a new semi-detached three-bedroom house being built by William Leech at North Lodge, just north of Chester-le-Street. The house was completed and we moved in April 1959.

The next two years were happy. My third daughter, Jill, had been born in February 1958 and as our house at Clough Dene had only two bedrooms, more space was needed. The new house at Chester-le-Street with a third bedroom was a big improvement.

I had bought my first car for £45, a 1938 Austin Big 7, at the end of 1958 and passed my driving test in March 1959 and everything seemed to be coming together at last with pleasant and friendly neighbours of a similar age. Wyn and Carole were at school nearby at Birtley and they took up ice-skating at Durham Ice Rink. I used to take them with a near neighbour and his daughter for group lessons every Saturday morning and after the lesson, we fathers joined them for general skating.

I also joined Chester-le-Street Cricket Club and began to enjoy playing at a higher standard in the Durham Senior League. There were many good players in the side, some of whom, like Tom Laws, I had known from school matches when Stanley Grammar School had played against Chester-le-Street Grammar School. There were

Author opening the batting with Geoff Taylor for Chester-le-Street at Sunderland in 1961

also some outstanding professionals in the league, including Alec Coxon, the former Yorkshire and England cricketer.

In the summer of 1960, I traded in my little Austin for a two and a half litre 1949 Riley, costing £240. It was a beautiful car with an enormous bonnet and leather interior and it gave me a good feeling to drive it, even if it eventually turned out to be unreliable. Wyn and Carole loved just sitting in it on the drive. One day, one of them managed to release the handbrake and the car rolled gently back into the drive gates, causing them no injury and little damage, but much embarrassment. Chester-le-Street was a pleasant place to live and for a time, all seemed well.

By the end of 1960, having completed my research and commissioned the full-scale effluent treatment plant at Brancepeth Coke Works, I had to start thinking about making a fresh start professionally. Several scientists who had joined the NCB at about the same time as I had were now Area Laboratory Managers. I had done some good and interesting work but it had taken me outside the main stream of career progression in the NCB and now that the carbonisation effluent treatment problem had largely been solved, it was hard to see where I might have a future in that organisation. It was an ill-defined feeling as I was happy at Chester-le-Street. I did not scan the pages of Situations Vacant consistently, and the advertisement that was to change our lives I saw by accident.

In the spring of 1961, I was painting the living-room one day and had spread pages from *The Observer* of the previous Sunday on the floor below where I was painting. As I came down the stepladder, I noticed the words 'Chemist and Bacteriologist' at the top of a box in the Situations Vacant section. Having read the details, I was immediately interested. The post was with South West Suburban Water Company, based at Egham in Surrey and I thought instinctively that that was the job that was right for me as my next career move. The description of the work seemed to fit my qualifications and sounded interesting, while the advertisement mentioned a starting salary of at least £1,500 per year, compared with under £1,100 that I was receiving from the NCB at that time.

I wrote a letter of application and was invited to an interview at the company's office at Egham on Wednesday 24 May 1961. Although my qualifications were appropriate, I had little experience in the field of drinking-water. The NCB supplied water to a fairly small number of houses in County Durham and as a result, I had done some bacteriological examination of water during my time at the Divisional Laboratory but I was well aware of the gaps in my knowledge. I borrowed a copy of the great book by Thresh, Beale and Suckling, *The Examination of Water and Water Supplies* and absorbed as much as I could on the long train journey from Newcastle to King's Cross in London on 23 May.

The company had arranged a room for me at what was in those days called the Pack Horse Hotel in Staines, so I had to cross London to Waterloo station for a train to Staines. The train stopped several times and as we left one station, I saw that its name was Ashford. There were a few moments of slight panic as the only Ashford that I knew was in Kent. As the train slowed for the next station, I wondered whether it would be Dover or Folkestone, but was relieved to see that it was Staines.

The interviewing panel the next day was formidable, led by the Chairman of the company, Leonard Millis (later Sir Leonard), an

Author (left) with Sir Leonard Millis

economist and barrister, and the Director of the British Waterworks Association (BWA). He had with him his Deputy Chairman, Sir George McNaughton (a former Chief Engineer at the Ministry of Housing and Local Government) and another non-executive director, Thomas Hawksley, a Consulting Engineer and member of a famous engineering family. The Chief Engineer of the company, Jack Brock-Griggs and the Company Secretary, Cyril Jordan, were also present, along with Dr Roy Hoather, whose consultancy, Counties Public Health Laboratories, had for many years been carrying out water examination for the Company.

South West Suburban Water Company had been formed in 1883 by an amalgamation of the Norwood Water Company that served Norwood and Southall in Middlesex, with the Sunningdale Water Company. It was one of about thirty statutory water companies that together supplied water to about one quarter of the population of England and Wales. Each company operated through its own Private Acts and Orders approved by Parliament. These, taken together with the provisions of the Water Act 1945, defined the responsibilities and the powers of the companies, including their area of supply. The statutory water companies raised their capital on the Stock Exchange through shares traded in the normal way, but had important differences compared with most other companies.

They were subject to limits on their charges set by the Ministry for Housing and Local Government (later known as the Department of the Environment and later still by various other names). They were also regulated by provisions in the Water Act 1945, limiting the amount that could be carried forward in their accounts and the amount that could be transferred to reserves. So they enjoyed considerable management freedom compared with the municipal sector of the water industry, but nevertheless were required to meet detailed statutory obligations. There were many good companies but critics did have a point when they argued that the system could lead to a comfortable style of management and to over-investment, the so-called 'gold-plated' investment that is sometimes seen in monopolies.

The other candidates being interviewed on that day in May 1961, were all working in the water industry and until that day, I had never even seen a waterworks, so I was not optimistic. The only question I remember being asked about my work for the NCB was from Leonard Millis. He asked, 'What can you tell the panel about the characteristics of Durham mine waters?' 'I'm sorry, but I don't know anything about mine waters as all my work has been connected with coal carbonisation and the treatment of effluents from that process.' I've never been sure whether the question was deliberately intended to tempt me to pretend to knowledge that I didn't possess, but whatever the reason, from the Chairman's reaction to my reply, I began to feel more confident.

I was offered the post and immediately accepted. Then, as soon as I left the office, I remembered that I had not discussed salary, so I asked permission to have a few more minutes with the panel. I told the panel that I had forgotten to raise with them the considerably higher cost of housing in the South West Suburban area than in County Durham and ask them if they could take that into account in setting my starting salary. Leonard Millis didn't hesitate. He said, 'We'll give you another 10%', taking the £1,500 per year in the advertisement up to £1,650. My relationship with my future Chairman had started well!

On 31 July 1961, I left Chester-le-Street in my Riley and drove to Ruislip, where my Aunt Grace and her family had moved from

Kenton and where she had offered to let me stay while the sale of our house in Chester-le-Street and the purchase of the four-bedroom house that we had bought in Ashford, Middlesex, were completed. The next day, 1 August 1961, I arrived at The Causeway, Staines, for my first day as Chemist and Bacteriologist for the South West Suburban Water Company.

In 1961, the company supplied water to about quarter of a million people in an area from Ascot and Bagshot in the west through Sunningdale, Virginia Water, Egham, Staines, Ashford, Stanwell and Feltham (including part of Heathrow Airport) to Southall in the east. The company abstracted water from the River Thames at Egham, where it received quite complex treatment before being pumped into supply.

The arrangement under which, for many years, the company had used Dr Hoather's firm of consultant analysts in London to carry out water examination of raw and treated water had been quite common in the water industry. However, although there could be no doubting the skill and experience of Dr Hoather's staff, the system suffered from the obvious drawback that response times were not as fast as the growing importance of water quality demanded. It was this that had led Leonard Millis to convince his Board that the company could not reasonably continue without setting up its own laboratory and recruiting a qualified chemist and bacteriologist.

When I arrived, I was shown a space in a former pumping station, which was to be the temporary laboratory, and invited to say what I needed to be able to start work. It was exciting to be given this responsibility and things began to happen quickly. At this stage, I shared an office with two young civil engineers, Geoff Moss and Chris Cotton. We got on well together, and they, along with the Chief Engineer, Jack Brock-Griggs, his Deputy, Gordon Hicks, and Wally Dobson, the Senior Assistant Engineer, all did everything they could to help me learn about the operations and the problems that arose from time to time.

Then, in October 1961, I appointed my first laboratory assistant, Sheila Quennell, who had just passed her 'O' levels at Sunbury Grammar School. She turned out to be outstandingly able and reliable and after a few years of part-time study for her 'A' levels, the company sponsored her to take a sandwich degree course at the newly created Brunel University at Hillingdon, where she took an honours degree in applied biology. When combined with the breadth of her experience of water examination, her degree made Sheila an outstanding water scientist, although her career wasn't always easy in the male-dominated water industry of that time.

The temporary laboratory soon took shape and by the end of 1961, we were carrying out a reasonably full range of water examination tests. Leonard Millis arranged a visit to the new laboratory by a group of scientists from the Water Research Association, fairly recently established at Medmenham, near Marlow, where I'd spent time sweeping up leaves during my service in the RAF. One of the scientists was Dr Ron Packham and he asked me about the work we were doing. I told him that we were building up our analytical programme and we were testing every day for a few determinands, including hardness. He asked how much the hardness varied from day to day. I replied, 'Not much.' Ron went on, 'And what do you do about it if it does change?' 'Nothing. There isn't anything we can do and it doesn't matter anyway.' 'Then why do you measure it every day?' asked Ron, not so innocently.

The truth was that we were doing the test because we were able to do it. That was another example of the need to think through the basis of the design of sampling and analytical programmes, to set alongside my coal-sampling experience at Norwood Coke Works when the sampler thought that we wouldn't want stones included with the coal samples.

In the autumn of 1961, the design of a new office block for the company was being completed. It had four floors and most of the third floor was shown as laboratory space. Again, I had a free hand in the design within the overall space available and one innovation that we introduced was the use of metal furniture beneath traditional wood worktops. In the spring of 1963, the new building was completed and the new laboratory occupied. By then, there was a good team of laboratory assistants being led by Sheila Quennell and I was spending an increasing amount of my time on trying to improve the water treatment processes.

Part of this required an understanding of the research being carried out at the Water Research Association (WRA). There were two teams there doing work of particular interest to me. One, led by Dr Derek Miller, was trying to find improved methods of filtration, while the other, led by Dr Ron Packham, was studying the processes of chemical flocculation and coagulation and I came to see both scientists as personal friends. I began to be invited to give technical papers on the work we were doing at South West Suburban on improving the water treatment. One such innovation was the adoption of an idea developed in the USA.

I used to scan scientific abstracts and one day, I saw a mention of a paper on the use of anthracite as a filter medium in rapid gravity filters. My NCB background probably increased my interest and I obtained a copy of the paper. The idea was to place a layer of relatively coarse but light anthracite on a layer of conventional fine but heavy sand so that better use was made of the depth of filter medium in the filter. It seemed to me to make sense and the authors reported good results so I telephoned a Coal Board friend and asked him if the NCB could supply size-graded anthracite suitable for this kind of use. A load of the material was obtained from South Wales and a layer of anthracite placed on top of the filter sand in one of the eight rapid gravity filters at Egham. The experiment was successful and all the filters at the company were subsequently converted to the two-layer system.

The Chairman of the water company, Leonard Millis, was Secretary General of the International Water Supply Association (IWSA) in addition to his main role as Director of the BWA. After a Board meeting in the spring of 1964, he told me that the Board had decided that the Deputy Chief Engineer, Gordon Hicks, and I should attend the sixth IWSA Congress to be held in June in Stockholm. I'd never been to an international conference and I could hardly believe that I was to fly to Stockholm and that the company would be paying.

We flew to Stockholm from Heathrow on one of the new BEA Trident jets for what was to be a memorable week. There were many interesting sessions at the congress and much to do outside the technical meetings. My former fellow students from Stanley Grammar School, Bart and Mary Hunter had given me an introduction to their old friend Captain Orrevik who lived in Stockholm and when I phoned him, he immediately invited Gordon Hicks and me to his home for dinner. He also arranged to take us to see the warship, the *Vasa*, that had recently been raised after sinking on its maiden voyage in the sixteenth century, and took us to see the village of Skansen on the outskirts of Stockholm. He and his family could not have been more kind, even when we showed our ignorance of their Swedish etiquette of drinking toasts at dinner.

I also discovered that the Woody Herman band was playing in Stockholm and went to hear them in a room that was so small that I thought the roof might be blown off. It was a truly memorable experience to hear musicians like the trombonist Bill Harris live, people that I'd listened to through records for so many years. During an interval, I even managed to find something to say to Sal Nistico, the great tenor saxophone player with the band at that time.

There were also two very special social functions that were part of the congress programme. The first was a trip by boat to Drottningholm Palace for a performance of a Pergolesi opera in the magnificent theatre of the Palace, followed by supper. The second was a splendid dinner in the Golden Hall of the Stockholm City Hall, a venue that was to become special to me thirty years later when I was appointed to represent the IWSA on the Nominating Committee for the Stockholm Water Prize. The week in Stockholm in 1964 was a really mind-broadening experience, which I expect was exactly what Leonard Millis had hoped.

Soon after joining South West Suburban Water Company, I met the Chief Clerk of the company, Bob Wire, whose brother Pat was Secretary of Laleham Cricket Club. Bob introduced me to Pat and I was invited to join the Laleham Club. In April 1962, I went to the ground and met Dick Faulkner who was Chairman of the Club and had just stepped down as first team captain after about fifteen years in the job. We got on well and I also met Alan Mason who had just been elected captain to replace Dick Faulkner. I was selected for the first team for the first game of the season at home to Turnham Green and for the second team for the Sunday game at home to Sunbury. We batted first on the Saturday and I walked around the field with John Swannell, a good cricketer and all-round athlete who played football for Corinthian Casuals at the time and later won many amateur international caps in goal for England while playing for Hendon.

John had played some cricket in the north of England while at university in Manchester and we discovered one or two common acquaintants. He asked me what number I was batting and I told him, 'Eleven'. He said that he'd have to try and do something about that and soon, I found that I'd been moved up the order to number seven. Eventually, we were all out for about one hundred and thirty, of which, Den Dancer who opened the batting made sixty-five, I made thirty-five and no one else made double figures.

On the next day, I made over fifty against Sunbury second team and thought that this southern friendly cricket was easy. It took a great many failures over most of the rest of the season to make me realise that the way the game was played in London Club Cricket was much nearer the approach in Durham League Cricket than I had imagined. It was another hard but valuable lesson in the dangers of making easy early assumptions.

In my last couple of years in Chester-le-Street, concerns had been growing among many people about the dangers of nuclear war. The first hydrogen bomb had been exploded at Bikini Atoll in 1954 and a few years later, the Campaign for Nuclear Disarmament (CND), had been formed. I joined CND and took part in a march to lobby the Labour Party Conference at Scarborough in 1960. At Easter 1961, I went to London with two colleagues from NCB Scientific Department to join the CND march from Wethersfield to London where we met the column of CND supporters who had marched from Aldermaston, west of London.

So when I moved to Ashford in the autumn of 1961, I looked for evidence of kindred spirits. I found an advertisement in the *Staines and Egham News* for a meeting in Staines Town Hall of the Staines group of CND and went along. I made some great friends there, including Norman Willis, who later became General Secretary of the Trades Union Congress. He and I did our best to stimulate discussion of the issues but also had a lot of fun together. Through Norman, I also became involved in local Labour Party affairs as the Willis family dominated Ashford East Ward Labour politics and it was hard to work with Norman in CND and not be part of local politics at the same time.

Soon after moving to Ashford, we found that Richmond Ice Rink ran Saturday morning classes for children on similar lines to those that Wyn and Carole had been attending at Durham. From then, every Saturday morning until they had passed all the examinations open to them without individual tuition, I drove Wyn and Carole to Richmond in the brand new Ford Popular car that had replaced my beloved, though unreliable, Riley in October 1961. They began to attend junior school at Spelthorne, within walking distance of home in Ashford and in 1962, Wyn won a place at Ashford County School, a mixed grammar school run on similar lines to my old school at Stanley. Her two sisters followed her there, Carole in 1965 and Jill in 1969.

All three did very well at what was an excellent school. Wyn had developed an interest in jazz and for her seventeenth birthday, I took her to Ronnie Scott's Club in Soho. It was wonderful to be able to take my grown-up daughter out in her first 'little black dress' to a famous jazz club to have dinner and hear the great tenor saxophonist, Ben Webster, as well as Dakota Staton, a very good jazz singer, performing that night. I even managed to make an opportunity to introduce Wyn and myself to Ben Webster at the bar between sets and he was very kind.

All three daughters took lessons in playing the piano, but Jill was probably the most talented musically. She took up the cello at school and music became an important part of her life. She continues to play regularly, both as a member of a good amateur orchestra and as part of a string quartet and her husband, Andy, also plays the cello well.

So life in the swinging sixties seemed pretty good. The children had settled well in their new environment; work was going well; cricket was good and there were good social contacts through work, cricket, CND and politics but domestically, signs of problems were growing.

There were tensions and disagreements at home over various things, such as the choice of schools for the girls, but I thought that these were the normal problems that arose in any marriage. Probably, I didn't give as much time as I ought to have done to considering whether the problems were more fundamental and whether anything ought or indeed could be done to improve matters. It's easy to tell oneself that everything is really OK and just muddle on, rather than to try to identify the underlying issues and attempt to address them. Things drifted for several years and suddenly came to a head in the United States at an international water conference in 1972.

CHAPTER 5

Into management and another new start

He is the rich man who can avail himself of all men's faculties.

Ralph Waldo Emerson, *Wealth* (1860)

IN 1966, IT BECAME KNOWN among the staff of South West Suburban Water Company that the Chief Engineer, Jack Brock-Griggs was planning to retire during the following year. Jack was a true gentleman in the Victorian tradition. He was part of the Brock family, who had owned the famous firework company. He had shot for England at Bisley and a relative had been awarded the Victoria Cross for his part in the Zeebrugge raid in 1917 during the First World War. Jack's social background and mine could hardly have been more different. In those circumstances, things could have been difficult and our relationship might have been distant, but in spite of the differences between us, we became quite close and he was always supportive of changes that I wanted to introduce. However, two examples may help to illustrate the gaps between us that we had to find ways of bridging.

I don't think that Jack had ever before worked closely with anyone from north of Watford or shopped anywhere other than Harrods, Fortnum and Mason or somewhere similar. One day, we were talking about the growth of supermarkets and I said something about the importance of the Co-op in northern communities.

Jack said, 'I've never seen a price for Co-op shares listed in the paper.' I replied, 'You won't have done because it isn't a conventional company – it's owned by its members.' His reaction was to ask, 'Then how does it raise capital?' I really didn't know the answer to that, but I said, 'I think each local retail Co-op is owned by its individual members and those retail Co-ops own the Co-operative Wholesale Society, so maybe capital is raised from the surpluses made by the retail societies.' It wasn't a particularly enlightening conversation on either side.

On another occasion, we were talking cricket and I said something about the ability that many bowlers have to make a cricket ball swing or swerve in the air. Jack commented, 'I can't see how it's possible for a cricket ball to do anything other than travel in a straight line'. I said, 'I know from bitter experience that some bowlers are able to make the ball swing a lot'. He just smiled and shook his head and it was no use trying to explain that a cricket ball is not a perfect sphere. But although communication between us was occasionally difficult he was always enormously kind and encouraging towards me and I could hardly have been luckier in my first boss in the water industry.

There was some speculation and internal manoeuvring among the other engineers about the succession. In the event, the Board decided on a major change of the management structure of the company. Fred Green arrived in September 1966 from Brighton Corporation Water Department to take over as the company's first General Manager when Jack Brock-Griggs retired. Fred Needham Green was an engineer but was in many ways quite different from Jack. Like Jack, he was a civil engineer, but he was also a mechanical engineer. His father had managed a gasworks in Wisbech and he had worked in the gasworks laboratory during school holidays, so he and I had something in common. When he arrived at South West Suburban, he had rather a long period ahead of him as General Manager Designate before he took full responsibility, so he spent a lot of time talking to all of us.

I remember him phoning me one afternoon and asking me to go to his office for a chat. He said that he'd talked to one or two of the engineers who all seemed to think that the company needed more staff. He asked me if I could think of any way that we could reduce the numbers of staff. I replied that I didn't know much about the overall organisation of the company, but I believed that we could halve the number of shift attendants from twenty-four to twelve.

Fred sat up straight and said, 'What makes you think that?' I explained that each shift consisted of four men. Two were designated as treatment attendants and two were designated as engine-drivers. Fred said, 'OK but what's your point?' I told him that the original role of the engine-drivers was to feed the boilers with coal so that they could raise the steam that drove the pumps, but that the coal-fired steam boilers had become redundant in the early thirties when the company had replaced the steam-driven pumps with electric pumps. The need for engine-drivers had disappeared then but the company had continued for over thirty years to replace them when they left. Fred roared with laughter and an always stimulating, although sometimes stormy, relationship began.

Fred Green took over as General Manager in September 1967 and less than a year later the Board agreed to his recommendation that I be appointed Assistant General Manager, while retaining my responsibilities as Chemist and Bacteriologist. It was an exciting time. There were suggestions that it was time to change the way the water industry was organised and most of us in the statutory water companies began to feel under threat. There was a Labour Government that was not well disposed towards the companies and powerful local government-based water supply organisations such as the Metropolitan Water Board made it clear that in their opinion, they ought to take over the companies.

At that time, something like one thousand municipalities had operational responsibility for sewage disposal, while about two hundred local authority joint boards and municipalities supplied water to seventy-five per cent of the population of England and Wales, with the remaining twenty-five per cent supplied by statutory water companies. There was increasing awareness inside and outside the industry of the need to improve efficiency and one way in which this was demonstrated was in Report 29 of the then Prices and Incomes Board.

The report described the water industry as low wage and low efficiency and recommended that both be raised through the introduction of work study-based bonus incentive schemes. The introduction of these schemes provided considerable work for several firms of management consultants and after receiving guarantees of no compulsory redundancy, the unions co-operated. In quite a short time, schemes were put in place at South West Suburban and throughout the industry. They were of variable quality, but they did make possible many of the improvements in efficiency and rewards sought by the Prices and Incomes Board.

The bonus schemes also created some interesting management problems. For instance, it soon became clear that some middle managers and supervisors, when faced with questions from employees about the calculation of their bonus were sending the employees to the work study officer for him to resolve the problem. This seemed to me to be wrong, as he had no direct operational management or budgetary responsibility. So I suggested to those managers and supervisors that they ought to ask themselves whether they really had a job if they were prepared to see their responsibilities discharged by the work study officer. If they didn't understand how the bonus scheme worked, it was up to them to find out. It wasn't popular but I thought and still do that it made an important point about the acceptance of responsibility.

An earlier development had been the introduction of legislation in the sixties requiring industries to make provision for training and later, new legislation on health and safety at work came into force. The water industry set up a training board in 1964 and it decided to establish several residential training centres. Manual worker training was offered at Flint House near Reading; at Melvin House (named after Robert Melvin, the Chairman of Bristol Waterworks Company) near Glasgow and at Millis House (named after my Chairman, Leonard Millis) near Derby. The training board also bought a large house at Tadley near Basingstoke, called Tadley Court, which became the Water Supply Industry Training Board headquarters and the management training centre for the industry.

The management training courses at Tadley were usually only one week long and I attended several in the sixties. One that made a lasting impression on me introduced me to the ideas of Fred Herzberg, an American management consultant. Briefly, he said that factors affecting work performance could be divided into two groups, genuine motivators and what he called 'hygiene factors'. The genuine motivators were recognition of achievement and the opportunity for new challenges following such achievements. Other factors like pay and conditions of work were the hygiene factors, on an analogy with hygiene in the health sense of the word. Good hygiene won't make us well if we are sick but it reduces the chances of us getting sick in the first place. Similarly, if the pay increase we expect and believe we deserve doesn't materialise, our performance is likely to be adversely affected but the genuinely motivational effects of a pay increase are essentially short-term. There are many examples of relatively well-paid boring jobs carried out by badly-motivated people where the truth of the theory may be seen. Understanding and applying the Herzberg principles can make a great difference to the way in which people react to their managers.

As we entered the seventies, my responsibilities at work were increasing rapidly at the same time as the water industry was itself changing and my family life began to come under more pressure. My management role at South West Suburban was expanding and professionally, I was becoming more involved in the wider water industry. For example, my Chairman, Leonard Millis, as Secretary General of the IWSA was keen for me to be part of the work of IWSA. Following my attendance at the IWSA Congress in Stockholm in 1964, I attended every IWSA Congress until the IWSA merged with the International Association for Water Quality (IAWQ), to form the International Water Association (IWA), after the Buenos Aires Congress in 1999.

In 1966, I went with Fred Green to the seventh IWSA Congress held in Barcelona feeling just a little more confident than I had been in Stockholm in 1964 in the presence of so many giants of the water industry. On this occasion, I attended a session on filtration and heard papers by two world experts, Professor Mintz from the USSR and Ken Ives (later Professor Ives) of University College, London. In Stockholm, I had been too frightened to say anything publicly, but by 1966, I had myself given a paper to a meeting of the Institution of Water Engineers on filtration through a two-layer bed of anthracite and sand, so in Barcelona I plucked up courage, and contributed to the discussion.

Afterwards, Ken Ives was kind to me when we chatted and subsequently he and I did some collaborative work on filtration, some of which led to us being joint authors with Dr Derek Miller from the Water Research Association of a paper to the Institution of Water Engineers that won an Institution Prize in 1970.

For a time, I became Secretary of the Special Commission on Pollution of Surface Waters of the IWSA. Case Biemond of the Netherlands, a former President of the IWSA chaired the Commission and I began to learn something of how water was managed and organised politically in other countries.

In 1969, I attended the eighth IWSA Congress, held that year in Vienna, and then was again invited by my Board to be a delegate to the ninth IWSA Congress in New York in 1972. For me, this really was a dream come true. Since childhood, I had been fascinated by the glamour of Manhattan. I'd grown up seeing pictures of skyscrapers such as the Empire State Building and the Chrysler Building in magazines and at the cinema. New York was also synonymous with jazz as the home of 52nd Street where the bebop of Dizzy Gillespie and Charlie Parker had blossomed in the forties.

The New York Congress was due to begin in early September 1972 and Leonard Millis asked Fred Green and me to help with the organisation. I became much involved in planning post-Congress tours, including the technical part of a tour to Rochester in New York State, followed by the Canada Centre for Inland Waters at Hamilton in Ontario and then Toronto. The travel arrangements were the responsibility of the American Express Company, which meant detailed negotiations with their people as well as with IWSA staff, and people at the various places hosting the visits.

A key member of the team in the IWSA London office responsible to Leonard Millis for the organisation of the Congress was Deborah Hyde. When she, Fred and I arrived in New York, we discovered that the Americans had changed many of the details of the plans that had been made in UK. This meant that there was a great deal of work to be done and Deborah, Fred and I worked long hours checking the new itineraries and amending all the handouts. Deborah and I got on very well and I soon realised that I was seeing her as far more than just a colleague. By the last week in September, we were all back in England and I came to the conclusion that I had to make a change, but the process turned out to be slow and painful for everyone.

I received a phone call on the morning of Sunday 22 May 1973 telling me that my father had died. He was relatively young, being only 68, but had been told some years before that he should give up smoking and for whatever reasons hadn't done so. I remember little of my father's funeral but I know that I wasn't able to give my mother the support that she needed until later.

Soon after my father's funeral, I moved temporarily into a room offered to me by a cricketing friend, Malcolm Phillips, who had a flat at Slough. Then, at the end of August 1974, Deborah and I moved into a new house on a large development at Heatherside near Camberley and began a permanent relationship that eventually became marriage in May 1983, a few weeks after my divorce was finalised.

The four or five years immediately following the autumn of 1972 contained much sadness for all of us involved. But they did lead to a future in which Deborah and I have enjoyed much happiness and in which my daughters and I have built a new relationship while they have developed a strong bond with Deborah.

Wyn had done well in her 'A' level examinations in 1969 and had read French and Spanish at Southampton University. She was taking her final degree examinations in the summer of 1973 when family problems were just about at their worst, which couldn't have helped her. Anyway, Wyn achieved a good honours degree and has had a successful career, becoming Deputy Head of a large comprehensive school at Yateley in Hampshire and taking an MPhil. She also became active in local politics and the arts and served as a member of Southampton Council for a number of years.

Carole was gifted academically and in sport. She played both tennis and hockey well and I remember watching her play hockey for Ashford Ladies. Unfortunately, an injury to her ankle cut short Carole's sporting career but she has kept her interest in sport. In 1972, she achieved good grades in her 'A' level examinations and went up to the University of Newcastle upon Tyne in October to read microbiology. Her choice had given me real pleasure because she was going to study a subject much the same as the bacteriology I had studied in the same place with some of the same lecturers.

A little later in the seventies, having taken her BSc at Newcastle in 1975, Carole took an MSc at Manchester for a statistical study of left-handedness. Then, in December 2002, she took an MA in counselling in the Social Sciences faculty at Manchester. She had had a difficult time bringing up her two daughters, Anna and Lauren, after the break-up of her own marriage and it was a great joy for Deborah and me to be there in the Whitworth Hall in Manchester in 2002 to support her and see her receive her degree. It was a bitterly cold day and after an early start from Hedley, Deborah and I only got seats in Whitworth Hall because Anna and Lauren kept places for us in the queue for people without tickets. They were just about frozen stiff. Afterwards, we took lots of pictures and celebrated over a jolly lunch with a bottle of champagne.

In 1976, having passed her 'A' level examinations, my third daughter Jill, left Ashford County School and went up to the University of Manchester Institute of Science and Technology (UMIST) to read biochemistry. She took her degree in 1979 but life was difficult for young science graduates at that time. Eventually, Jill joined the Inland Revenue and in spite of devoting an enormous amount of time to her daughter, Philippa, and her son, Robbie, as well as keeping up her cello playing, she has now qualified as a tax inspector.

I've always been proud of all my daughters and loved them very much. It's also true that my temperament and my many involvements meant that I didn't display my emotions as overtly or as frequently as some fathers did, but I enjoyed doing lots of things with them. Of course, I could and probably should, have done more, but I also think that it is easy to be too protective and Wyn, Carole and Jill have each in their different ways turned out to be reasonably balanced and well-rounded people, each successful in her own way.

The upheavals I've described in my domestic life had some temporary repercussions in my professional life. In 1973, South West Suburban Water Company had merged with a neighbouring company, the Woking Water Company, to form North Surrey Water Company and Fred green became General Manager of the new company. In the 1970s, for all the talk of the swinging sixties, social attitudes in the water industry remained conservative and I became resigned to failing to succeed Fred Green as General Manager of North Surrey Water Company. That began to change towards the end of 1976 as speculation started on the date of Fred's retirement.

By that time, I had accepted responsibility for running a joint laboratory providing water examination services to the Sutton District Water Company as well as to North Surrey. This came about largely because Leonard Millis was Chairman of both companies and Geoffrey Edwards (later to become Chairman of Thames Water Authority) was Deputy Chairman of both. I was invited to join the Sutton Board for lunch before each Board meeting and at the December 1976 lunch, two things happened that showed that my position had improved.

At one point, Leonard Millis asked one of his non-executive directors, Colin Spens, how he had become a civil engineer. Colin had been Chief Engineer at the old Ministry of Housing and Local Government and had a well-deserved great reputation. Colin explained that he had been offered a place at Cambridge to read mathematics but had met the Professor of Civil Engineering at University College, London at a Garden Party in Kensington given by his mother and had been persuaded by him to switch to University College and engineering.

Leonard then turned to me and said, 'Tell us how you became a chemist, Jack.' 'Well, there weren't too many garden parties attended by professors of any kind in the mining village in County Durham where I grew up so I can't match Colin's story.' 'But', said Colin, 'you've done very well with a lot of responsibility as Head of the Joint

Laboratory.' Leonard then came in and said, 'Don't be silly, Colin. He thinks he should be Chairman of ICI, just as I think I should be President of the Bar Council.' Although I knew that Colin was a genuinely kind man who hadn't intended to be patronising, I was extremely grateful to Leonard.

That same day, as lunch ended and just before the Board meeting began, Geoffrey Edwards took me to one side and told me that Fred Green would be retiring as General Manager of North Surrey Water in 1997. He told me that the North Surrey Board would be confirming my appointment as General Manager Designate at the meeting the following week and he congratulated me. It was perhaps indiscrete of Geoffrey to tell me before the meeting and, indeed before Leonard had spoken to me, but I was delighted to be told and my appointment was officially announced a few days later. I don't think that Leonard ever knew what his Deputy Chairman had done.

CHAPTER 6

Standardisation and special friends

The proper office of a friend
is to side with you when you are in the wrong.
Nearly anybody will side with you
when you are in the right.

Mark Twain, 1935

D R EDWIN WINDLE TAYLOR was recognised as a world figure in water quality when he telephoned me early in 1973. He was medically qualified as well as being a barrister and was Director of Water Examination at the Metropolitan Water Board that supplied water to most of London. I had earlier joined old friends Len Bays, Tom Palin and Tom Waterton when I became a member of the Water Quality Committee of the British Waterworks Association, of which Windle was Chairman. Windle had been very kind in introducing himself to me, a new member, at my first meeting of the Society for Water Treatment and Examination at Great Yarmouth in 1961 and gradually we got to know each other. His call in 1973 was to tell me that British Standards Institute (BSI) was setting up a new committee to look at standardisation of water quality analytical procedures and that he'd put forward my name as a possible member.

In his biography of the great nineteenth century scientist, James Clerk Maxwell, (*The Man who Changed Everything*, John Wiley and Sons, ISBN 0-470-86171-1) Basil Mahon describes Maxwell being asked by the British Association for the Advancement of Science to look at the wide variety of units that had developed for the measurement of electricity and magnetism. In 1863, Maxwell and Jenkin produced a paper for the Association's Committee on Electrical Standards that recommended a complete system of units. These were later adopted almost unchanged as the first internationally accepted complete system of units. So it could be argued that James Clerk Maxwell was the father of standardisation because less than forty years after that paper, in 1901, the first British Standards

Committee met and just after the Second World War, in 1947, the International Standards Organisation (ISO) was formed.

The BSI Committee that I joined was called Environmental Protection Committee 44 and in the way of BSI, immediately became known as BSI EPC 44, Water Quality. Dr Trevor Rees from ICI chaired it initially and a little later, Dr Stella Patterson from the Department of the Environment succeeded him. In early 1974, at a meeting in the United States, which I did not attend, it was agreed to set up a Committee of the International Standards Organisation based in Geneva to cover the same basic remit as BSI EPC 44. This Committee was identified as International Standards Committee 147, or ISO TC 147, Water Quality, and it held its first meeting proper in London later that year at the splendid old offices of BSI in Green Street, off Park Lane in London. Six Sub-Committees were set up and I became a member of the Sampling Sub-Committee, designated ISO TC 147, SC6 with Trevor Rees as Chairman. It was given the responsibility of developing standards for the design of sampling programmes. It was not the most glamorous posting in the world of standards but it was and is a subject of fundamental importance that interested me and I was pleased to be part of this new international initiative.

My interest in sampling sprang originally from a short course in statistics at King's College as an undergraduate, when I had been struck by the fact that no analysis can have a greater accuracy than that of the least accurate measurement. Experience had shown me that that was something that was often forgotten or not even understood, as the anecdote that I related earlier about coal sampling at Norwood Coke Works illustrated.

Clearly, in that incident, the sampler had not understood that the main purpose of his sampling was to provide a truly representative sample of coal to enable the laboratory to measure the ash, sulphur, etc content of the coal so that the required blend of different coals could be fed from the coal washery to the coke ovens.

In the summer of 1975, there was a meeting of the parent ISO TC 147 Committee and the various sub-committees in Budapest. It was my first visit to a country behind the Iron Curtain and was an exciting experience. The old part of Budapest had many beautiful buildings reminiscent to me of Vienna. We stayed in the old part, in the Hotel Gellert where the meeting was held, a splendid old building with baths fed from natural hot springs. For some reason, there was a small parade by Soviet troops each morning outside the hotel that, for me, added an air of incongruity and even a little menace to the scene. There were many social events, including receptions, a concert and a visit to the ballet to see a memorable performance of *Electra*.

Many aspects of Hungary seemed strange, not least the fact that it was possible to buy a wide range of luxury Western goods if one were able to pay in hard currency, such as US dollars or pounds sterling. Although I could understand the reasoning behind it, there still seemed to me to be a strong whiff of hypocrisy about it. Our Hungarian hosts were most welcoming and hospitable and it was interesting to meet Hungarian and other East European scientists face to face.

One of the social opportunities offered to us was to join the graduation ball at Budapest University. Although the dances were different – I had to learn to dance the czardas – the general atmosphere was noisy and a little drunken in much the same way as I would have expected at a British university. The party broke up at about 4 a.m. and after a couple of hours sleep, we were on our way at 7 a.m. for a coach trip. After lunch at a collective farm, we continued our journey, eventually reaching Tokay in the east of Hungary where we visited the famous wine cellars and sampled some of their contents, including the famous dessert wine of Hungary, Tokay Aszu.

At the end of this meeting of the Sampling Sub-Committee, Trevor Rees resigned from his roles in BSI and in ISO, having retired from ICI. I was appointed Chairman of the BSI Sampling Committee, and at the next ISO meeting in Copenhagen in December 1976 I became Chairman of ISO TC 147 SC6. Some time later, I was appointed to chair the main water quality committee of BSI, known then as EPC 44 on the retirement of Stella Patterson.

My Chairmanship of the ISO Sub-Committee continued for almost twenty years, through meetings in many parts of the world, including Copenhagen, London, Ottawa, Cologne, Helsinki, The Hague, Tokyo, Paris, Berlin, Stockholm, Vienna and ISPRA, near Milan. We produced a number of good sampling standards and I made many good friends. Indeed the ISO Committee became a kind of international club where our relationships were based on individual mutual respect rather than on our employing organisations. For example, although Dr Windle Taylor had retired from the water industry in 1974, he continued to serve on the ISO Committee for many years, providing liaison with the IWSA.

Windle's attitude to life belied his age. His wife often rang me before an international meeting to ask, 'You will look after Windle, won't you?' I used to say, 'Yes, of course I will'. I really should have said, 'I'm the one who needs to be looked after when I'm away with Windle'.

A meeting of ISO TC 147 SC6 took place in London in the summer of 1978, not long after I had been appointed to succeed Fred Green as General Manager of North Surrey Water Company. BSI asked whether any of the British members of the Committee could arrange some hospitality. No one from the large Water Authorities volunteered so I asked my North Surrey Chairman, Leonard Millis if the company might offer something. He immediately agreed and the outcome was a splendid reception for the delegates at the Vintners' Hall in the City of London.

Vintners' Hall is one of the most beautiful of many beautiful livery halls in London and Sir Leonard received the guests formally with Lady Millis. He wore his robe and badge of office as Master of the Worshipful Company of Plumbers and there was an excellent buffet with entertainment by a West Indian steel band. The delegates were much impressed by the occasion and my British colleagues and I felt that North Surrey Water had upheld the reputation of the UK among our international guests.

During the ISO meeting in 1985 in Tokyo, Windle Taylor and I took time off and flew to Hiroshima for the day. It was terrifying and awesome to visit the museum directly beneath the point at which the first atomic bomb exploded in August 1945 and be reminded of the appalling consequences for the people of that city. But apart from the pictures in the museum, it was difficult to imagine what it must have been like in the immediate aftermath of the explosion, especially as the whole city had been rebuilt.

In 1987, Windle proposed me as a Fellow of the Royal Institute of Public Health and Hygiene and I became a member of the Council, of which I shall say more later on. Windle died in 1992 and I was surprised and flattered to receive a telephone call from his son, a surgeon in Plymouth, asking me to give the eulogy at Windle's funeral at Golders Green. I can only surmise that Windle had left a request to that effect, but however it came about, it was an honour to pay a tribute to one of the great men of the water industry. On the other hand, it was an occasion that reminded me of the speed with which once well-known people can be forgotten because there were only a handful of people from the water industry present to remember a man who had been one of the most influential leaders of the industry of his generation.

Among many other good friends made through International Standards was Dr Sybille Schmidt from Leverkusen, who has been for many years (and still is at the time of writing in 2005) Chairman of the main ISO Committee, ISO TC 147. Sybille represented DIN, the German standards organisation, on the Committee and was always an effective and fair Chairman. In March 1996, during my year as Master of the Worshipful Company of Plumbers (of which, again, more later), Sybille made a special journey from Germany to be my guest at the Plumbers' Annual Banquet in Mansion House in the City of London. I was honoured by her presence. In October 2003, I was delighted to be invited by Sybille to attend a dinner in Cardiff as a guest of ISO TC 147. There had been some changes in membership but many old friends remained and it was a typically warm and friendly occasion.

On my retirement from the chairmanship of ISO TC 147 SC6 and BSI EPC 44, I was presented with a BSI Distinguished Service Certificate to mark my twenty years of work on water quality standards. As John Boon, my old friend in the Water Companies Association, said, when it was announced that he had been appointed OBE, 'These awards don't come with the rations', and I was therefore touched to receive the certificate from my peers as a mark of recognition.

Another member of the ISO Sampling Committee was Professor Heinz Bernhardt from Siegburg near Bonn in northern Germany. He led the German delegation and at first, our relationship was severely formal. I was always 'Mr Jeffery' and he was always 'Professor Bernhardt'. Then, quite suddenly, there was a rapid thaw. We became 'Heinz' and 'Jack' and one of the closest friendships of my adult life began to develop.

Heinz Bernhardt grew up in Dresden in eastern Germany and was living there as a sixteen year-old boy in February 1945 at the time of the devastating air raid by the RAF. After we became friends, we sometimes talked about the war and his memories of the raid and the firestorm that followed. At first when the subject came up, I was somewhat embarrassed but Heinz said that he felt no bitterness and that the attack had to be seen in the context of the war generally and the raids by the Luftwaffe on Coventry, Liverpool, London and other cities.

As the Soviet army approached Dresden, Heinz left his home and made his way to Switzerland. He went to university there and later moved to Siegburg, where he became one of the best-known water scientists in the world. His reputation was such that for a number of years before the reunification of Germany, he was able to travel freely to and from East Germany to lecture at the University of Dresden whilst at the same time being a Visiting Professor at the University of Aachen in West Germany.

Problems could arise in ISO because of the mandatory nature of ISO standards in Germany once they were adopted by the German Standards body, DIN. ISO standards are not mandatory in the UK and I don't know of any other country where they are. Inevitably, that made the German delegates inclined to be cautious. That wasn't necessarily a bad thing and Committee members from other countries understood the situation and were usually sympathetic. Heinz and I worked well together, sometimes bringing Sybille Schmidt into our negotiations in resolving such occasional differences between the German and UK delegations.

Heinz was also active in IWSA and we began to meet from time to time in IWSA meetings. At the fortieth anniversary meeting of IWSA in Nice in 1987, Heinz and his wife Pia were guests at a small dinner party that I hosted as Chairman of the Water Companies Association and he made a charming speech. Soon after that, there was a reorganisation of the Editorial Board of *Aqua*, the journal of IWSA. Len Bays, then Secretary General of IWSA, got agreement to setting up a new group with Heinz Bernhardt as Chairman of the Board and I was asked to become a member. Over the next seven or eight years, Len Bays, Heinz and I operated as a three-man working party of the Editorial Board.

We met twice a year and reported to meetings of the full Editorial Board held in conjunction with the IWSA Congresses held every two years. Most of the meetings of this small working party were held in Heinz's home just outside Siegburg or at his summer home overlooking Lake Lugano in Switzerland near the Italian border.

Typically, Len Bays and his wife Sheila would fly to Cologne or Lugano with Deborah and me on a Friday afternoon and return to London on Sunday. In December, Siegburg was always attractive with the market in the square dressed for Christmas and in autumn we sometimes visited Klusserath in the Moselle valley where Heinz's friend Franz Regnery had a vineyard.

At Klusserath, we used to stay at a small *gasthof* and have a private wine tasting of the wines of Franz Regnery in Herr Regnery's house. After a number of bottles, Frau Regnery would produce open sandwiches of steak tartare and cheese and then it was back to the tasting. It would have been fine had we approached the tasting in the classic manner of rolling the wine around our palates and then spitting it out, but for most of us, that seemed a waste of good wine. As a result, our walk back from Regnery's house to the *gasthof* was often somewhat unsteady! On one occasion, I think we 'sampled' twenty one different wines, including one or two outstanding *ausleses*.

Our meetings in Lugano were always in summer and I have many happy memories of dinner on the terrace of the Panorama Hotel on a steep hill overlooking the lake from the Italian side or on the terrace of Heinz's summer home. Heinz loved the music of Johann Strauss and Deborah has some wonderful photographs of Heinz and me waltzing on the terrace after an enjoyable dinner accompanied by several bottles of wine!

Heinz and Pia also visited England on a number of occasions and stayed with Deborah and me several times at the house in Curley Hill Road, in Lightwater where we had moved from Camberley in the autumn of 1979. They came to stay at the time of my sixtieth birthday party at Great Fosters Hotel in Egham in March 1990 and they also visited the Lake District with us when Heinz and I were making arrangements for a joint scientific meeting between IWSA and the Freshwater Biological Association.

I last saw Heinz in December 1995, when he attended a meeting in London. He stayed with us at the house in Chobham in Surrey that was our temporary home from October 1995 until April 1996 while our new home was being built at Hedley on the Hill in Northumberland. He was suffering from prostate cancer and was obviously very ill. Sadly, he died a few weeks later in January 1996.

Few people are aware of the standardisation work of ISO, its committees and the national standardisation bodies such as BSI in the

UK. But the results of this work play an important part in the lives of all of us. Just one example may illustrate this. In recent years, it has become commonplace to see references to ISO 9000 or later ISO 14000 and compliance with these quality assurance standards gives considerable reassurance to all of us that the organisations concerned are trying to meet high standards in the work they do and the services they provide.

It was a great privilege to be allowed to contribute to this work for such a long period and to make so many friends and meet so many interesting people in so many parts of the world.

CHAPTER 7

Changes in the water industry

He knows nothing and he thinks he knows everything.
That points clearly to a political career.

George Bernard Shaw, *Major Barbara*, 1905

B Y THE END OF THE SIXTIES, it was clear to most of us that the
pressure for organisational change in the water industry was
growing. The Labour Party that had threatened to nationalise the
water companies had lost the 1970 election, but the new Conservative Government, led by Edward Heath, soon gave signs of planning
a reorganisation of the industry. When that reorganisation came with
the Water Act 1973, the changes were far-reaching. All of the
municipally run water suppliers and sewage disposal bodies were
brought together in ten regional water authorities, which were also
given regulatory powers to control abstractions of water and the
discharge of effluents. This meant that each authority had complete
control of and responsibility for the water cycle in its region. There
were, however, several anomalies.

One was that although there was already in existence a Water
Resources Board dating from 1963 with a responsibility for managing
water resources nationally, the mechanism through which it might
enforce transfers of water between regions was far from clear, if such
a provision existed at all. This anomaly was exacerbated by the
privatisation of the Water Authorities by the Water Act 1989 and
responsibility for the management of water resources nationally still
remains somewhat confused.

Another anomaly concerned the twenty-eight statutory water
companies. At the time, it was generally believed in the water
industry that the original draft of the 1973 Water Bill provided for
the companies to be brought into the new authorities that the Act
was to create. At a late stage of drafting, at a meeting of back-bench
Conservative members of Parliament, it is said that it was pointed out
to ministers that there was something odd about a Conservative
Government being seen effectively to nationalise the only part of the

water industry that had survived successfully in the private sector. As a result, the Bill that was eventually brought before Parliament by the Secretary of State, Peter Walker, was amended to exclude the companies from the legislation on the grounds that they were already generally efficient.

A little later in the seventies, a new Labour Government threatened to amend the law so as to incorporate the companies into the regional water authorities. The Government had a small majority and needed Liberal Party backing for such new legislation. After strong lobbying by the Water Companies Association, the Liberals refused to support abolition of the statutory water companies. It was commonly believed at the time that retention of the statutory water companies was a condition of the 'Lib-Lab' pact that allowed the Labour Government to retain office.

But perhaps the most serious problem was not recognised until later. In the early seventies, the organisation set up by the Water Act 1973 was seen as an ideal model for water management in most parts of the world, not least in the United States. The principle of integrated water management based on river basins that the Act established was seen as taking us away from the bad old days of uncoordinated management of water resources and pollution control. However, what gradually began to be recognised was that the Act had created ten authorities that were in effect both poachers and gamekeepers.

For example, as regulators, they set the discharge consent limits for sewage works' effluents, but as operators of sewage treatment plants, the same organisations were given the responsibility of monitoring and meeting those limits. Pressures from Government on the prices charged by the authorities and on their ability to borrow almost inevitably led to problems and gradually sewage effluents became recognised as the most serious component of river pollution across the country.

The United Kingdom had joined the European Community in 1973 and in 1978, the first European Drinking Water Directive was agreed. It was to have far-reaching consequences for the UK water industry, although as usual in the UK, it was some years before these began to become clear. To most of us concerned with water quality it seemed obvious that the numbers in the Directive were derived from the World Health Organisation Guidelines for drinking water quality with which we had been familiar for many years. We knew that by and large we complied with the WHO Guidelines and we were confident that we supplied drinking water as good as any in the world.

In the mid-eighties, our complacency was shattered when, under threat of legal action against the Government in the European Court, Government lawyers pointed out a crucial difference between the WHO Guidelines and the European Drinking Water Directive. The limits in WHO Guidelines are based on lifetime exposure to the concentrations of the determinands listed and therefore, compliance with the Guidelines is usually interpreted in terms of quarterly or annual means.

The lawyers forced us all to recognise that although the numbers in the Directive were much the same as those in WHO Guidelines and were clearly derived from them, the limits in the Directive were described as 'Maximum Admissible Concentrations' and therefore, we could not claim to be complying on the basis of average concentrations. This had profound implications for the water industry and for the Government. The huge capital expenditure associated with meeting limits for each determinand for each and every sample rather than on the basis of averages was an enormous blow to the Government and the water industry.

The Regional Water Authorities were under political pressure to keep down charges and to reduce their borrowing from a Conservative Government that saw reducing taxation as a main priority. So where was the capital to be found? The Government led by Mrs Thatcher thought the unthinkable. It began to consider ways of privatising the water industry and I shall deal with that subject later in the chapter.

On the retirement of Fred Green from North Surrey Water Company in September 1977 and my appointment to succeed him as General Manager, I began to attend meetings of the Council of the Water Companies Association (WCA). The Council consisted of representatives of all twenty-eight member companies and the Chairman was Sir John Cockram. Sir John had been Chairman of the Association for something like thirty years. He was an able man, a powerful personality and as Treasurer of the Public Works Congress Council, a long-standing colleague of my Chairman at North Surrey, Leonard Millis, who was Director of the Public Works Congress.

At that time, WCA Council meetings were held in St Ermin's Hotel in Westminster and they began, I think, at 11.30 a.m. At my first meeting, I was a little nervous in the presence of so many

Geoff Ingham, the author and Sir Leonard Millis

well-known leaders of the water industry, but I needn't have worried. The proceedings were almost entirely formal and the meeting was over before noon. I soon found out that Sir John and senior members of the Council were disappointed if the Council business could not be dispatched within about twenty minutes and therefore, questions and comments from new Council members were not encouraged. Nevertheless, there were ways in which members were assessed and in time, Sir John became a good friend.

The WCA had a number of more specialist groups – technical committees, working parties, etc, – and I became part of the informal group of General Managers of seven water companies whose areas of supply were largely within the area of Thames Water Authority. The other companies represented were Colne Valley, Rickmansworth and Uxbridge Valley, Lee Valley, Essex, East Surrey and Sutton and District. I already knew Geoff Ingham, the Managing Director of the Sutton and District Company, well through my earlier management of the Joint Laboratory serving that company and North Surrey and because we shared the same chairman, Leonard Millis.

All seven companies collected the sewage disposal charge on behalf of Thames Water and were bound by decisions taken by the regional trades unions/employer negotiating bodies. As Thames Water dominated the employers' side, it was important that the representatives of the companies were clear about the views of their colleagues before they got into a formal meeting. Sometimes it seemed that we were faced by not one, but two groups of opponents in such meetings!

Responsible to WCA Council was the Executive Committee of the Association. Most of the real discussion and decision making in the WCA took place in the Executive Committee and I soon found myself elected to membership of it. Recognition of the need for change in the water industry was reflected among many of the younger members of WCA Council, but there was also a powerful group of more conservative senior members. They argued with some justification that the statutory water companies had survived for a great many years by doing a good job, adopting a low profile and avoiding controversy – what some of us in the younger group referred to as 'keeping our heads down'.

In 1979, the Conservative Party under the leadership of Mrs Margaret Thatcher won the General Election. The immediate reaction of many senior people in the statutory water companies was that this would lift the threat of nationalisation of the companies or of their incorporation into the regional water authorities. But it soon became clear that Mrs Thatcher did not recognise many sacred cows and the attitude of the WCA Executive Committee began to change as it realised that one threat had been replaced by a challenge to the water companies to demonstrate their effectiveness and efficiency. One of the first signs of this was the decision by the Committee to support a proposal to set up a performance indicators sub-committee. Ron Slater, then General Manager of Mid Kent Water Company was appointed to chair it, and I became a member. The remit of the group was to develop indicators through which companies could compare their efficiency with that of other companies and thus find ways of improving efficiency all round.

For example, company A might be more efficient than company B in its use of energy, and company B more efficient than company A in its use of manpower, while company C might be better in each category than either of the others but less efficient by different criteria. By comparing such indicators, companies began to produce genuine improvements, although there were, as ever in such exercises, some who quickly developed great expertise in devising plausible explanatory factors for poor indicators rather than concentrating on attacking the problems that were exposed.

The idea that managers in a monopoly industry ought to be prepared to try to demonstrate their efficiency and effectiveness was somewhat ground-breaking at the time. It was an important development for companies wishing to improve and an important political signal from the WCA and its member companies to Government and others.

At about the same time as interest in performance indicators began to grow, questions began to be asked about various aspects of the role of the WCA and the way in which it operated. It was proposed that the WCA hold a conference to give directors and managers of all the companies the opportunity to discuss a wide range of aspects of water, from technical and administrative or financial matters to the organisation of the industry. Sir John Cockram, who had been Chairman for many years, was strongly opposed to the idea but the decision was taken to go ahead and as a result, Sir John's position was weakened.

Within a fairly short time, the WCA Council decided that chairmen should be elected for a three-year term and in 1981, John Boon was elected to succeed Sir John. John Boon had been Vice Chairman for a number of years and was an ideal person to take over because he had the respect of the 'old guard' as well as of most of the younger members. John was Managing Director of East Anglian Water Company, a small company in Great Yarmouth and was himself a larger than life character. He was a part-time farmer and was liable to turn up in London for a meeting with a brace of pheasants in a cold box for one of his friends.

John became an enthusiastic supporter of the WCA conferences. In fact, if I had to choose one word to describe John Boon, I think it would be 'enthusiastic'. He took the WCA through a tricky transition period with great skill and played a big part in establishing the statutory water companies as a force to be reckoned with in the water industry through his participation in national discussions with leaders of the water authorities and with senior politicians and civil servants.

In 1984, John Boon stood down as Chairman of the WCA and was succeeded by Maurice Lowther, at that time Managing Director of Newcastle and Gateshead Water Company. The idea was that someone would be elected at the same time as Deputy Chairman to serve in that position for three years and then become Chairman. I had not thought much about the election, so was surprised and flattered when I realised that I was being talked about for the post.

Just before the meeting at which the election was to take place, John Boon took me to one side and said, 'Gordon Spencer (General Manager of Essex Water Company, the biggest of the companies) will retire next year. He's been a great servant of the WCA and it would be a nice gesture if he were made Deputy Chairman in his last year as a member of Council. If you would propose Gordon as Deputy Chairman this year, I'll propose you as Deputy Chairman next year'. I'd worked with Gordon when he was Chairman of the WCA Technical Committee and we'd been part of a small team that gave evidence on research priorities to the House of Lords Committee on Science and Technology, so I was happy to agree. Gordon was elected for one year in 1984 and in 1985 I became Deputy Chairman of the WCA.

Maurice Lowther was a highly effective Chairman of the WCA. Like John Boon, he had infectious enthusiasm and could be an inspiring speaker with considerable self-confidence. Maurice never seemed to hesitate when he was speaking publicly and always sounded as though there could be no doubt that he was right. His brand of non-stop action-man leadership was just what was needed to lift the members of the Council of the WCA at a time of great uncertainty for the companies. In reporting to a meeting, he often began by saying, 'My feet never touched the ground' and another of his favourite quotations was the so-called Chinese curse, 'May you live in interesting times'. Some of the less reverent members of Council took bets on how long it would be before we heard one of those expressions in a speech by Maurice.

During the years between 1984 and 1987 when Maurice was WCA Chairman, the Government's proposals for the privatisation of the water industry slowly crystallised. By the time of the Annual General Meeting of the Association in 1987, the political battle lines were fairly clearly drawn. We knew in principle the way in which the Bill to be presented to Parliament would be drafted and were analysing the possibilities and potential threats to our companies. At the Council meeting that followed immediately after the AGM in July 1987, I was elected Chairman of the Water Companies

Association with John Browning of Bristol Waterworks Company as Deputy Chairman. Together with Michael Swallow, a lawyer who was Director of the WCA and his Deputy, Valerie Homer, we entered one of the most hectic and exciting phases of my life. The next three years were indeed, in the words of Maurice's Chinese curse, 'interesting times'.

We quickly realised that the WCA would need expert specialist advice in several areas. Andrew Kennedy, a lawyer with Stanley and Simpson North (later Beachcroft Stanley) in the City had had long links with the water companies and was a director of East Surrey and Sutton water companies so we felt well served on the legal side.

However, we decided that we needed to appoint merchant bankers to represent us and that we also needed public relations advisers. The Regional Water Authorities had all appointed advisers some time earlier, so most of the better known merchant bankers were not available to us, but we talked to Brown Shipley and felt satisfied that they would be able to give us reliable and good advice. For public relations advice, we went to Burston Marsteller, a well-known international firm.

The Green Paper published by the Government in 1986 had recognised the principle that as a privatised water industry would be virtually a total monopoly, it would need an effective system of regulation but the Paper drew criticism from a number of sources, some unexpected. The original proposal was to privatise the Regional Water Authorities essentially as they stood, including their environmental regulatory responsibilities. There was a superficial logic to this. The system of integrated water management introduced by the Heath Government in the Water Act 1973 had attracted much praise around the world. Therefore, the Government was understandably reluctant to be seen to be changing that system too much soon afterwards. The Paper also rejected the statutory water company (SWC) model of privatisation, describing it as an old-fashioned method of involving the private sector. Instead, it proposed an economic regulatory system based on control of price increases with no limit on profits made within that system of price control.

The result was almost universal opposition. Trades unions were predictably worried about possible job losses and changes to working conditions, but the reaction of the Confederation of British Industry (CBI), was more surprising to the Government. For a time, I was a member of the Council of the CBI and represented the WCA on the Water and Effluent Committee of the CBI. With a little help from me, the CBI quickly realised that if the regulatory powers of the Authorities were transferred to the privatised bodies, the result would be a situation that would be unacceptable to their members. They saw a possibility of one plc having the power to take legal proceedings against another plc for its failure to meet, for example, a limit set in a consent to discharge, while at the same time failing to meet consent limits for its own sewage discharges but escaping prosecution. It seemed to me at the time that real genius had been required to produce a proposal that succeeded in uniting against it the CBI, the trades unions as well as the Opposition in Parliament.

Eventually, a new Secretary of State for the Environment, Nicholas Ridley, accepted that the regulatory duties of the Water Authorities could not remain with them after privatisation. He put forward a broader regulatory system for the new Water Service PLCs (WSPLCs) and SWCs. At first, all of the RWAs, except Severn Trent under the chairmanship of John Bellak, opposed this but the WCA gave support and gradually the new proposals became accepted.

Three new regulatory bodies were proposed for the water industry and the Water Act 1989 brought them into being, as follows:

1. A new environmental regulator to be called the National Rivers Authority (NRA). After a fairly short time in existence, its responsibilities were widened and its name was changed to the Environment Agency (EA).
2. An independent regulatory organisation to be called the Drinking Water Inspectorate (DWI), to monitor compliance with the requirements of the EU Directive as applied in UK Drinking Water Regulations. Michael Healey, a senior engineer in the Department of the Environment, was later appointed to be the first Chief Inspector of the DWI.
3. The Office of Water Services (OFWAT). It was eventually established under its first director, Ian Byatt (now Sir Ian), to administer the economic regulatory process and protect the interests of consumers (or as we began to learn to call them, 'customers').

A Bill was introduced into Parliament and Michael Howard MP, then Minister of State at the Department of the Environment, was given the responsibility of piloting the Bill through its Committee stage. The Bill had to be published in two volumes and I have been told that it was, at least at the time, the longest Bill ever taken through Parliament. A principal reason for this was the complexity of the regulatory system demanded by the privatisation of an industry that, in any particular geographical area, was and is an almost complete monopoly.

Having become Chairman of the WCA in July 1987, I was almost immediately involved in the political process. At the time, we in the WCA were extremely fortunate to have access to advice from two senior parliamentarians with strong links to the Association. Sir William Elliott had become Lord Elliott of Morpeth in 1985 having been MP for Newcastle upon Tyne North from 1957 to 1983, an Opposition Whip in the sixties and Chairman of the Parliamentary Select Committee on Agriculture, Fisheries and Food from 1980 to 1983. He had been President of the WCA for many years and on his retirement from that post in 1986, he continued to help whenever he was asked.

His successor as WCA President was Sir John Page, who served as MP for Harrow West from 1960 until his retirement from Parliament at the 1987 General Election. Jack Page has a different personality from that of Bill Elliott but both had vast parliamentary experience and a great commitment to the water industry generally and to the WCA and the SWCs in particular. They were both well-known in Parliament and respected across the political spectrum, so they were tremendous assets to the WCA. There is no doubt in my mind that access to the political wisdom of Bill Elliott and Jack Page helped us in the WCA (and also the Government) to get a lot of things right that we and Government would otherwise probably have got wrong.

As the Council of the WCA consisted of representatives of all twenty-eight SWCs there was no shortage of opinions on the right way to proceed. Council members were almost all General Managers or Managing Directors of their companies.

We were all used to running our own companies and more accustomed to making business decisions and negotiating with trades unions than dealing with professional politicians. At times, some members of Council, such as David Parr, then Managing Director of Essex Water Company, expressed the view quite forcefully that the SWCs were not getting a fair deal because I was not taking a sufficiently strong line with the Minister and his civil servants. David was an influential member of the WCA Executive Committee and he and one or two others seemed to think that the WCA was in a much stronger bargaining position than was in fact the case.

At one point, I decided that the way to create awareness of the political realities was to find a way of involving the WCA Executive Committee directly with ministers. A meeting was held over lunch in a private room at the Selfridge Hotel in London. The Secretary of State, Nicholas Ridley, the Minister, Michael Howard and their top civil servants all attended and the six members of the WCA Executive Committee were present, together with the Deputy WCA Chairman, John Browning, Managing Director of Bristol Waterworks Company, Michael Swallow, the WCA Director and me. I arranged the seating plan so that I sat in the middle of one side of the oblong table with Nicholas Ridley on my right, with John Browning opposite me with Michael Howard on his right. I put David Parr on the right of Michael Howard to give him every opportunity to impress the Minister. Michael Howard dealt with the rebels on my committee exactly as I had expected and I had much less criticism subsequently.

There was another amusing episode during the lunch involving the Secretary of State and the Minister. At one point, Nicholas Ridley said, looking at Michael Howard, 'Of course, we make policy and our civil servants carry it out'. While Michael Howard was smiling at this remark, Nicholas Ridley appeared to re-consider, and then said to him, 'Come to think of it, I make policy and you carry it out'. The Minister continued to laugh and I'll never know whether Ridley planned the incident or it was just another example of him playing things 'off the cuff'.

From the start of the passage of the Bill, one fact was obvious to us in the WCA. The Bill was primarily designed to privatise the Regional Water Authorities set up under the Water Act 1973. Therefore, it concentrated on the mechanisms for the transfer to the private sector of the publicly owned Regional Water Authorities (RWAs). As a result, not enough thought had been given to the quite separate issue of the transfer of the SWCs from one set of statutory controls to an entirely different regulatory system.

Most of the subsequent difficulties that arose between the Minister of State, Michael Howard, and the WCA arose from this initial cavalier attitude of the Department of the Environment to the companies. The significant role already played in the water industry by the private sector was one of two important differences between the privatisation of water and that of other industries privatised by the Government of Mrs Thatcher.

There was another important difference. Unlike other utilities like gas and electricity, water had never been nationalised, so the Government did not own the assets it was selling. This bit of background to the privatisation of water is an interesting example of applied politics.

The Water Act 1973 had created the RWAs by a simple transfer of the assets and responsibilities of the municipal water and sewage undertakings to the new bodies. During the Committee stage of the Bill, there were mutterings by some local authority leaders that the local authorities had paid for the assets that were being transferred to the RWAs and that local authorities should receive compensation for the take-over. There was, of course, never any chance of the Government paying compensation to municipalities. However, local authorities were told that the Act would provide for there to be a majority of local authority representatives on each of the RWA Boards and therefore, local authorities would still effectively be in control.

The Water Act 1973 did include such a clause but it turned out to be a temporary guarantee. In 1983, yet another Water Act removed the provision for local authority members to be in the majority on the Boards of the RWAs. Mrs Thatcher had become Prime Minister in 1979 and soon decided that the RWA Boards were not as efficient and effective as they ought to be. Part of her analysis was that there was too much local authority influence and she wanted to see a more business-led approach. So the right to nominate a majority of RWA Board members was removed from local authorities and a new breed of RWA Chairman began to be appointed.

Men (they were all men) like Roy Watts at Thames Water were recruited from industry and they were told to manage the RWAs like commercial businesses within the restrictions on borrowing imposed by the Treasury through the Public Sector Borrowing Requirement (PSBR). There were a few criticisms but by and large local authorities accepted the change. This was partly because the RWAs were still seen as being in the public sector and partly because, after ten years, many of those local authority leaders who could have remembered the compensation arguments in 1973 had probably retired.

So four years after removing the requirement for a majority of RWA Board members to be local authority nominees, the Government was now proposing to sell to the private sector assets that it had taken from municipalities without compensation and transferred to the new RWAs in 1974. Amazingly, there was little reaction to this from local authorities. Perhaps they just didn't appreciate what was happening!

The detailed problems that had to be resolved are not part of this account although they may be for another occasion, but one over-riding issue is worth recording. The Government was bringing two totally different groups of water utilities under the same system of economic regulation and for a long time, the Government and its civil servants did not fully appreciate the significance of this.

Author with his cousin, Ron Jeffery, at a Mansion House Banquet

For some time in the eighties, the RWAs generally had seen their borrowing limits reduced, forcing them to generate capital from revenue through increases in charges. The SWCs on the other hand, were still operating within a legal framework under which their shares were seen as almost equivalent to Government fixed interest stock and so their financial gearing was not of concern to the City. This made it easy for the companies to borrow to fund their capital expenditure, thus keeping their charges typically below the charges of the RWAs.

The method of economic regulation proposed by the Government was commonly described as price control (as opposed to the system of profit control that had long applied to the statutory companies). However, it was, in fact, a system of control of price increases, something rather different. In a system where control on profits was being removed, one of the criteria by which the City was going to judge the new companies was gearing ratios. The fact that the statutory water companies had high gearing meant that the cost of borrowing in the new regulatory system automatically increased. Ministers and civil servants underestimated the significance of these largely technical matters. John Browning, Michael Swallow, Valerie Homer and I sometimes felt that no one was listening.

On two separate occasions I wrote to the Minister, Michael Howard, pointing out that SWCs would soon have to announce their charges for the coming year. I told him that it was important that I was able to give my members some assurance that the Government recognised the problems its proposals were creating for the SWCs, and had solutions in mind. I received no reply and so in the early weeks of 1989, I authorised the publication of a press release saying that the privatisation proposals of the Government meant that SWC charges would have to rise by up to 50%. That announcement became the major item in most Sunday newspapers that weekend and the Minister appeared on television at Sunday lunch-time saying that the SWC statement was outrageous and that he would be seeking an urgent meeting with me.

On Tuesday afternoon, two days later, I left the WCA offices in Great College Street with Michael Swallow to walk across the road to the Houses of Parliament. It was a new experience to have television cameramen walking backwards in front of me as we crossed the Embankment and entered the House, where we were taken to

Michael Howard's political office. He was seated behind his desk and there were two straight-backed chairs in front of it. It was a little like two schoolboys going to see the headmaster. Several senior civil servants were lounging on a settee. The atmosphere was, to say the least, tense.

The Minister asked me how I could possibly justify the WCA press release. I answered by taking him through the implications for my own company, North Surrey, of the Government's proposals as they then stood. The clear advice from our merchant bankers was that North Surrey was unlikely to survive if the proposals were adopted and we did not raise our charges dramatically. I knew the figures for North Surrey well and when I'd finished, Michael Howard made no comment on my analysis but said that 'it wasn't good for any of us when we had a public disagreement'. I replied, 'I agree, but we felt that as companies were near the date when they had to announce their charges for next year and as we'd had no reply to our letters, the Association had no alternative but to go public to support our member companies'.

The Minister then asked if we could issue a joint press release after this meeting. I answered, 'Yes, of course, provided we can find a form of words that is acceptable to us both'. He picked up a piece of paper and said that he had a draft, and I replied, 'I thought you might'.

The Minister then read a short document that basically said that we had met and that the Minister had sought an explanation of the WCA press release. I said, 'It's all right as far as it goes, but if it is to be a joint release, won't it seem strange if it doesn't include any reference to the WCA response to your criticism?' Michael Howard thought for a few moments and then asked if I would be happy if he added, 'The Chairman of the WCA explained the background to the statement?' I said that that would be acceptable and soon afterwards, Michael Swallow and I left the meeting.

Just over an hour later, I had a call from Jeremy Warner of *The Independent*. He was one of the few journalists to make a serious attempt to understand the details of water privatisation and he said, 'I've just seen the joint press release and you don't seem to have given anything away'. I asked, 'Why do you say that?' Jeremy said, 'Because the release ends with your response to the Minister and doesn't mention any further comeback by the Minister'. I just replied, 'I can't add anything to what the press release says.' I felt quite pleased with the outcome.

The practical solution that eventually emerged after much argument was an agreement by the Department of the Environment that in the first years of the new system of economic regulation, charges of the SWCs would be allowed to increase by more than those of the WSPLCs. This device allowed a transition from high debt/low charges to lower debt/higher charges over several years for the SWCs, enabling them to compete in a fair way with the WSPLCs. Within a short time of the 1989 Act coming into force, the SWCs converted from their traditional statutory framework to either plc or limited company status. In the new regulatory system, they became known as Water Only Companies (WOCs).

In 1989, price limits for the water industry had been fixed for ten years by the Secretary of State, but the Act gave the Director General of OFWAT power to undertake a review of price limits after five years. It was not long before Ian Byatt announced his intention to exercise that power. The review was vastly complicated and required an enormous amount of technical and management input. Those of us in the WOCs continued to stress the unfair position that we believed we occupied and although Ian Byatt never conceded the point, I think that in practice, he found ways of acknowledging our special problems. After the 1994 review of prices, it was clear that the world had moved on and that the WOCs had to be judged by the same criteria as the WSPLCs.

Those years that I served as Chairman of the WCA between 1987 and 1990 were stimulating, frustrating and exciting. They were a tremendous education in the workings of democracy. Not only did I meet and debate with Ministers and senior civil servants frequently, but I also met many senior politicians from the Opposition parties. My overall impression was that only a tiny minority of the politicians I met had any understanding of or, indeed, interest in the details of the privatisation proposals.

Ministers had been given the task of getting the Bill through the House of Commons and didn't want to hear anything that suggested the need for further consideration. Opposition members at the Committee stage of the Bill were always ready to meet me but with rare exceptions were only hoping that I might tell them something that they might be able to use to embarrass Michael Howard. That was clearly unlikely to help achieve a level playing field for my members. At the end of the process, I felt that the WCA had played

The author with Frank Muir, launching North Surrey Water Aid appeal

an important role in making the Water Act 1989 and the regulatory system that it put in place far more effective and workable than it would otherwise have been.

The water industry changed dramatically in the ten years after privatisation. I think that most of the changes were for the better in terms of service to our customers. Water quality standards improved considerably from a starting point that was already good and generally speaking, the regulatory system worked well. There were big improvements in efficiency across the industry, which meant that the price increases, although large, were less than they might have been had the regulatory standards been met in a public sector framework.

One valid criticism was that the newly-privatised water companies were allowed to put in place share option schemes for their senior people that were a licence to print money. That was because the financial structure that was created for them was specifically designed to make their flotation attractive to investors, so those senior managers would have had to be wholly incompetent had they failed to be profitable. They generally did a good job but when the scale of their rewards became known, the industry as a whole attracted a great deal of bad publicity that contributed to the poor perception of the industry by the public through much of the nineties.

CHAPTER 8

Research

Learning is its own exceeding great reward
William Hazlitt, *The Plain Speaker*, 1826

ONE OF THE MANY PARADOXES in my life is that having had to
make do with a poor first degree at university, a fair proportion
of my career was spent doing applied research, working with
researchers or directing research, work that was usually the preserve
of those with a much stronger academic background than I had. For
example, as I've described, after eighteen months with the National
Coal Board as a coke works chemist, I worked for over six years on
a successful programme of research into the biological removal of
phenols and thiocyanates from the effluents from coal carbonisation.
Later on, I had a considerable involvement with Water Research
Centre (later WRc plc) and the Freshwater Biological Association.

When I moved to South West Suburban Water Company in 1961,
most people at the company saw the job of chemist and bacteriologist
as largely one of routine water examination. One of the civil
engineers was heard to describe my post as that of the bottle washer.
That began to change quite quickly as far as I was concerned when
I realised that the civil engineers at the water company were not
much interested in water treatment. Jack Brock-Griggs and his
Deputy Engineer, Gordon Hicks, had published a paper on work
they had done on chemical coagulation and sedimentation of water
drawn from the River Thames. The plant had been commissioned at
Egham in the early fifties but by the sixties, the engineers were
generally content to leave the operation of the water treatment plant
to Bob Wells, the excellent Treatment Superintendent who had
grown up on the job.

Bob was a great character with considerable knowledge and
experience of operating the treatment plant. I began to spend a lot of
time listening to him and learning how he made judgements about
matching chemical dose rates to changes in raw water quality and the
detail of backwashing filters. For example, he had a microscope in his

107

office and from early spring through the summer months, he examined samples of River Thames' water every day, looking for changes in algal activity that might make it necessary to change the treatment regime.

It was clear that he thought that the treatment plant might be operated more efficiently, but was understandably reluctant to take any risks without the support of his managers. He and I began to experiment with lower chemical doses and the use of a 2-layer filter with a layer of coarser anthracite on fine sand. I related this work to costs of chemicals and energy used in backwashing the filters and to the possibility of increasing the throughput of the plant. So the research was strongly focused on improving the efficiency of the plant and reducing costs.

One day, as part of trying to understand how the treatment plant was supposed to work, I asked one of the company's senior engineers, 'What's the specification that the filters are supposed to meet?' He replied, 'A million gallons of water per day, per filter.' I said, 'Yes, but what does the specification say about removal of suspended solids?' His answer was, 'Nothing,' to which I commented, 'So the filters would meet the specification if we'd forgotten to put in the sand?' He clearly thought that it was a stupid question, but if his answer was correct, it was amazing to think that those filters had been designed and built without any real thought having been given to the quality of the raw water they would be treating or to the quality of filtered water they were intended to produce. Perhaps more likely, the original design by the manufacturer and supplier of the filters had been based on knowledge of the quality of the water to be treated, but the company's engineer had just never thought about it.

My work on water treatment led to several invitations to present papers and in the discussion on one of the first of these, I was taught an important lesson. I gave the paper at a meeting of the Society for Water Treatment and Examination and among the audience was Dr Palin, the Chemist of the Newcastle and Gateshead Water Company. Apart from being recognised at home and abroad as a major figure in water science at that time, Tom Palin was also famous as the only water scientist that any of us knew to have made money beyond his salary from his skill. He had developed a method in his own time for producing reagents in tablet form for measuring chlorine in water and had successfully patented the process. The income per tablet was small but when his method was widely adopted in the United States for use by the water suppliers and by swimming pool operators, the gross income became considerable.

In the discussion on my paper, Tom Palin said with a smile that he'd found my paper very interesting but he couldn't help wondering how the customers of South West Suburban Water Company had ever received a safe supply of drinking water before I joined the company! He made his comment without any sign of malice but I took the message very much to heart.

Soon after I began this piece of applied research, the Chairman, Leonard Millis, said to me, 'You ought to join the Freshwater Biological Association'. I didn't need to be told twice and I became a member in the mid-sixties. I'd heard of FBA, but knew little of the work done at its laboratory at the Ferry House, across Lake Windermere from Bowness. Leonard told me that he was Treasurer of FBA and took me to visit the recently opened River Laboratory, near Wareham in Dorset.

The head of FBA at that time was Hugh Gilson and there were many famous freshwater scientists connected with the Association, including people like Professor Tony Fogg and David Le Cren. FBA scientists were among the best in the world in the fields of algology and freshwater fish, and had a huge scientific reputation much of which arose from their work in African lakes over many years.

I began to attend FBA scientific meetings, especially the summer meeting associated with the AGM, held at the Royal Zoological Society at Regents Park in London. This was a special occasion in the sixties. It was followed by a dinner in the Society, after which the aquarium of the Society was opened for a private tour by FBA members.

The Council of FBA was a mix of elected members and representatives of various bodies such as the Worshipful Company of Fishmongers, the Salmon and Trout Association and the Institution of Water Engineers and Scientists (IWES), now the Chartered Institution of Water and Environmental Management (CIWEM). I had become a Fellow of the Institution and in about 1980, the then President of IWES, Maurice Lowther (later to be my immediate predecessor as Chairman of the WCA), asked me if I would represent IWES on the Council of FBA. I agreed and soon, I was asked if I would become Treasurer. It was a special honour for me to fill a post that had been held by my Chairman and I think that Leonard Millis was pleased to see his protégé in that position.

When it had been founded between the wars, many of the scientists were people once described as 'of independent means' and external funding was not an issue. This situation changed gradually and by the time I became Treasurer, FBA depended for most of its funding on the Natural Environment Research Council (NERC). The Rothschild report on research had effectively recommended that the focus of research funding should be on 'relevance' rather than on excellence and this was becoming more and more accepted.

This worked against FBA because its scientists concentrated on fundamental research and it increased the importance of the relationship of FBA with NERC. At that time, the emphasis at FBA had always been on excellence and little effort had been made to apply the results of research. There were even some scientists around at Windermere at the time who almost resented any suggestion that their research might be applied and many of these had tenure, so there was a problem, not only in FBA but also in many research associations and university departments.

Although my first reaction to Rothschild had been to support the argument about relevance, I gradually began to doubt whether it is possible to be precise about defining relevance. My own applied research on improving water treatment would clearly be seen as relevant. Much of the work done by FBA researchers over previous decades would not, and yet it had proved enormously important to the water industry, for example, in improving the management of reservoirs such as those of the Metropolitan Water Board (now Thames Water plc).

Sir John Gray was FBA President in the mid-eighties. He was a distinguished marine biologist working at the Marine Biological Association Laboratory at Plymouth and he and I, as FBA Treasurer, had many meetings to try to obtain adequate funding from NERC. Eventually, in 1988, Sir John decided that he had had enough of battling with civil servants about money and resigned as FBA President.

Soon afterwards, to my complete surprise, Professor Gwyn Jones, the Director of FBA, phoned me and told me, 'I've discussed Sir John's resignation and the possibilities with senior FBA staff and taken soundings among Council members and we all agree that we would like you to become our President. Will you do it?' I replied, 'My scientific reputation doesn't come anywhere near the standards of past Presidents. I'm not sure that I'm the right person to maintain the reputation of FBA.' He very kindly said, 'You're recognised as combining a good scientific background with financial awareness. We think that you're the right person to handle the difficult politics of our financial situation.'

So in 1988, I began a seven-year spell as President of FBA. It was a great honour and privilege to preside over an organisation with such an outstanding scientific reputation, at home and internationally. There were many difficult meetings with NERC staff such as Dr Eileen Buttle and Sir John Krebs (later to become Chairman of the Food Standards Agency). They had huge problems themselves in NERC in trying to maintain a satisfactory research effort across a wide range of science at a time when the overall funding that they were allocated by Government was always under threat. I think that maybe my appreciation of their problems helped me to build relationships with them based on trust and mutual respect that worked for FBA at the time.

Soon after I retired from the position of FBA President in 1995, the Council of FBA invited Deborah and me to be guests at a dinner at the Royal Society in London. My successor, Sir Fred Holliday, former Vice-Chancellor of Durham University and Chairman of Northumbrian Water, made a charming and generous speech before presenting me with a decanter engraved on one side with my name and my years as President and on the other side, with the freshwater shrimp that is the emblem of FBA. It was a memorable occasion.

During the eighties, I began another research involvement when I was appointed to represent the WCA on the Council of the Water Research Centre (WRc). WRc carried out research, mainly applied, into a wide range of water and waste-water problems. It had come into being after the Water Act 1973 by merging the Water Research Association (WRA) and the Water Pollution Research Laboratory (WPRL). WRA had been created in the fifties to carry out operational research for the water supply utilities and as I've mentioned, I'd done some collaborative work with scientists there in the sixties. The water supply companies, municipalities and joint boards, owned WRA.

Research into sewage and industrial waste-water treatment had been carried out since just after the First World War by the WPRL, part of the Department of Scientific and Industrial Research (DSIR) and therefore a Government laboratory. WRA was based at Medmenham, near Marlow in Buckinghamshire and WPRL had laboratories at Stevenage in Hertfordshire.

The newly formed WRc was, as WRA had been, a company limited by guarantee. It was funded mainly by subscriptions paid by its owners, the Regional Water Authorities , Scottish Authorities, Northern Ireland and the Statutory Water Companies, but also earned money through contract research, including some for the Department of the Environment. Joining the Council of WRc in the eighties was interesting, as it was a period of such rapid change. At first, there was much discussion of the level of subscriptions and of research priorities. As it became clear that the Government was serious about privatising the water industry, the possible implications of such a change had to be considered.

It was realised that it would be difficult for Government and environmental regulators to continue to award research contracts directly to WRc after most of its owners became privatised in the way being proposed. After much debate, it was decided that WRc could only have a future if it found a way of breaking the direct ownership link with the water utilities. Michael Rouse, the Director of WRc, had asked me if I would stand for election as Deputy Chairman of the Council of WRc and following my election, I began to work with the Chairman, Bernard Henderson, who was also Chairman of Anglian Water Authority, later Anglian Water plc. It was decided that in order to ensure the independence and impartiality of WRc, we should have to find a way of privatising it. Conversion to plc status via a staff buy-out seemed to be the right way to achieve this.

Bernard Henderson and Michael Rouse asked me to chair a group to recommend a share structure and that proved to be a difficult task. The senior management team of WRc, led by Michael Rouse, obviously wanted a staff buy-out on favourable terms, while on the other hand many leaders of the water industry were against giving up control of assets that had been bought by the industry, and certainly not at a give-away price.

After much haggling, we came up with a proposal that was accepted by both sides. It involved creating two classes of shares, one class to be held by the privatised water companies and the Scottish municipal water undertakings, with the other class held by the members of WRc staff who bought the shares. The first class of shares would carry no say in the policies or management of the company save in the event of a proposal for the winding-up of WRc plc. It was a device that allowed the privatisation of WRc to go ahead and made possible contracts from Government and regulatory bodies. But it was not a satisfactory permanent solution and after a few years, the share structure was changed to an orthodox single class of ordinary shares.

Bernard Henderson stepped down as WRc Chairman when it became WRc plc in 1989 and John Sadler was recruited from the John Lewis Partnership as non-executive Chairman. Bernard and I became non-executive Directors, Michael Rouse was appointed Managing Director and David Field, John Moss and Alan Halder became executive Directors. Things appeared to go reasonably well for a time, but in the autumn of 1992, there was effectively a mutiny. Field, Moss and Halder went to John Sadler and told him that they could no longer work under Michael Rouse. John Sadler asked me to meet him and it was clear that he was not supporting Michael. I said that in the situation he described it was our duty to support Michael, certainly at least until he had had a chance to give his side of the story.

I left the meeting believing that Sadler had accepted my argument and that nothing dramatic would happen for a while. It was my hope that the Chairman would be able to talk some sense to the group that had approached him and avoid the obvious threat to the longer-term existence of WRc plc. A day or so later, I left the UK to give a paper in Toronto to a meeting of the American Waterworks Association. I arrived at my hotel in Toronto at about 7 p.m. on a Sunday evening and was given an urgent message to call Michael Rouse at his home, and although it was by then after midnight in England, I made the call. Michael said that John Sadler had met him on the previous Friday afternoon and told him of his meeting with the other executives. The fat was truly in the fire.

An extremely difficult period followed and predictably, the outcome didn't fully satisfy anyone. Eventually, John Sadler resigned as Chairman and Michael Rouse ceased to be Managing Director, replacing Sadler as non-executive Chairman. Of the three executive Directors, John Moss had been the only one who had shown any real appreciation of the danger to WRc and the only one ready to compromise, and Bernard Henderson and I persuaded the Board to make John Moss Managing Director. It was arguable that all four executives should have gone, but that would have meant exposing at a sensitive time the whole sorry mess to the industry, Government and regulators, with possibly dire consequences for applied water research in this country, for WRc plc and for the staff who had invested in the company.

After a fairly short period, Michael Rouse resigned as WRc Chairman when he was appointed Chief Inspector at the Drinking Water Inspectorate on the retirement of Michael Healey, the first Chief Inspector. This was a post that suited Michael Rouse very well and he did an excellent job there. For a few months, I became Chairman of WRc plc with the task of trying to get the company back on the right track and of finding a new Chairman.

We appointed to the post a recently retired senior manager from ICI, Ralph Hodge. The following year, Ralph became Chairman of Enron Europe, an appointment that at the time did not seem relevant to his position at WRc. I remained a director of WRc and Bernard Henderson retired from the Board and was replaced by Sir William Stewart. Bill Stewart had been an outstanding scientist and had for some years been Scientific Adviser to the Cabinet Office, a key post in the setting of UK science policy from which he had fairly recently retired. He and I had known each other a little a few years earlier as fellow Council members of FBA and he brought to WRc a considerable knowledge of research policy as well as contacts with a wide range of influential scientific administrators.

The new Board gradually began to identify the things that needed to be done and John Moss quite quickly showed that he had the ability to change things round, but WRc plc was operating in a difficult market. Many of the water utilities had in the past placed individual research contracts with WRc but after privatisation, there was an increasing tendency for the newly privatised companies to wish to carry out their own research.

To some degree, I think this was part of a desire among a number of executives of the companies whose earlier experience had generally been in the public sector to show the world how macho they had become post-privatisation. On the other hand, there was some good news when the water companies agreed to give up their special powers on dissolution of the company, making it possible to change the share structure to a single class of ordinary shares, a structure much more appropriate to a plc.

Life continued to be far from easy for WRc in the second half of the nineties. As well as the water companies cutting back on their research expenditure, the regulators and Government departments were similarly slow to commission new contracts. There were several promising overseas initiatives, including an office in Philadelphia in the United States and a partnership in Italy, but none really took off in the way we hoped.

When Enron decided to diversify from energy into water, it seemed for a time that this might lead to some commercial opportunities for WRc. Enron set up a subsidiary, Azurix, to operate in the water business and soon made a successful offer to buy Wessex Water in England. This allowed Enron to claim a substantial presence in the British water industry and gave the company a base from which to try to obtain international contracts. WRc had good links with Wessex and a visit by WRc was arranged to Enron headquarters at Houston in Texas to discuss possible cooperation between WRc and Enron. As Ralph Hodge was Chairman of Enron Europe as well as of WRc, he was careful to avoid any direct involvement in the discussions because of his obvious direct conflict of interest, so I made the trip with WRc MD John Moss and David Field, the executive director responsible for technical matters.

We flew to Philadelphia to meet the people from our US subsidiary, WRc Inc, and to consider what we ought to focus on at our meeting with Azurix. Having roughed out our tactics, we turned these ideas into a PowerPoint presentation on the flight from Philadelphia to Houston. On arriving at our hotel, we went straight into a meeting with senior Azurix directors over dinner and made our presentation the next morning.

The whole occasion was amazing. Although two senior managers from Wessex were present, they were not based in Houston and none of the American directors had any personal knowledge of water. Additionally, they seemed to me to be lacking even the most elementary understanding of the politics of water in their own country. The water industry in the United States includes some investor-owned utilities run on similar lines to the former statutory water companies in England and Wales but it is dominated by the municipalities. Many of these, like New York City, Chicago and Los

Angeles, are very large indeed. Local politicians run those municipalities and there is little enthusiasm for the private sector although a group of private sector management consultants seemed to do quite well by producing reports saying that the municipal undertakings could not in any circumstances be managed more efficiently. 'Privatisation' is for many in the US water industry a dirty word. In this environment, Azurix executives talked glibly to us about their confidence that they would win the contract to supply water services to the city of Birmingham in Alabama.

When I added the political situation in Alabama and the general municipal attitude to the private sector in the US to the fact that I did not see any black executives in the Azurix offices, I left Houston with little confidence in the likelihood of Azurix succeeding. I was not at all surprised when after quite a short time, Azurix ceased to exist and Wessex Water was sold again.

In the midst of all this, the one good thing was that the balance sheet of WRc plc remained sound, with assets that comfortably exceeded liabilities. The company began to look to move into different areas and became less close to the water companies. As a result, my influence reduced and I retired from the Board of WRc in 1999 after almost twenty years' involvement with the organisation.

My research links resulted in one other remarkable experience when I was invited to visit South Africa in 1994. After many years of isolation of South Africa, the apartheid regime had eventually ended and for the first time, free elections had been held. Nelson Mandela became the new South African leader and soon had a successful meeting with John Major who had succeeded Margaret Thatcher as British Prime Minister. One of the outcomes of that meeting was an agreement to explore the possibility of cooperation between South Africa and the UK in scientific research.

The Chancellor of the Duchy of Lancaster, David Hunt, was the Minister responsible for science and he was asked by the Prime Minister to take a small team to South Africa to follow up his agreement with Nelson Mandela. Sir William Stewart was Scientific Adviser to the Cabinet Office and so it fell to him to suggest members of the team to accompany David Hunt, and I received an invitation to join the group. After a briefing meeting in Whitehall about twelve of us flew to Cape Town and began a fascinating few days of visits and meetings. We visited the University of Cape Town and a research station nearby and then flew to Johannesburg and on to Pretoria. There, we visited the University and the Environmental Research Institute as well as spending a night at a research station in the savannah north of Pretoria.

At Pretoria University, I renewed acquaintance with an old friend, the Professor of Microbiology, Willie Grabow, who had served with me on ISO water quality committees. Willie took me to his home and he and his wife then entertained me to dinner. That was my first introduction to the security measures that, certainly in those early days after the end of apartheid, were commonplace in white communities. Willie and his wife were far from being extreme right-wing racists but they were genuinely apprehensive. On several subsequent visits to South Africa, including a visit in 2004/05 with Deborah to watch the test matches at Cape Town and Johannesburg, I sensed that things generally are improving in many ways although there is no doubt that enormous problems still exist.

After a dinner in Johannesburg for our tour group in January 2005, a (white) former test-cricket selector made a speech that was highly critical of official policies in his country on positive discrimination in sporting selection policies. He was speaking to a group of white middle-class visitors from the UK and I guess that he assumed that he was speaking to a sympathetic audience.

While I agree that there are some good legitimate arguments against positive discrimination, it is not a simple issue in a country emerging from such a difficult past. Whilst listening to the speech, I couldn't help wondering whether the speaker had taken the same view of positive discrimination in the apartheid years. Then, the discrimination was absolute and it was totally impossible for outstanding cricketers such as Basil d'Oliviera to play cricket for the country of their birth unless they were white.

I think that scientific research has a special place in bringing together people of widely different cultures and backgrounds. Individual scientists have their fair share of human frailty but the principles of the scientific method of testing hypotheses against observed facts make it harder to support prejudices in debate with one's peers. My experience of meeting people from many different parts of the world has convinced me that we all have many more things in common than those things that divide us, and that the things we have in common are much more important.

CHAPTER 9

The French Connection

How can you be expected to govern a country that has two hundred
and forty-six kinds of cheese?

Charles de Gaulle, *Newsweek*, 1 October 1962

MY LONG INVOLVEMENT with the International Water Supply
Association had given me an awareness of the two big French
water companies, Compagnie Générale des Eaux and Lyonnais des
Eaux. Many of their staff presented papers and contributed to
discussions at technical sessions of the IWSA.

When the possibility of water privatisation began to be actively
considered, the WCA decided to look at the way in which the
French involved the private sector in the management of their water
industry. In planning a conference to be held at Windsor in 1985, the
WCA included in the programme a session on the French water
industry and Jean-Pierre Tardieu and Jean Claude Banon of Compagnie Générale des Eaux were invited to speak. Jean-Pierre was a
major figure in the IWSA at the time and I had met him occasionally
at IWSA meetings. Jean Claude was younger and had not long been
with Compagnie Générale des Eaux. Both had an engineering
background, but Jean Claude also had a business qualification and had
worked in business in New York. For me, it was the start of a long
involvement with them both.

One day in 1987, I had a call from David Kinnersley asking me to
have lunch with him. David was an economist who, in 1974, had
been the first Chief Executive of North West Water Authority. He
had then moved to the National Water Council, where, amongst
other things and before becoming an independent consultant, he
played a major part in the establishment in the early eighties of the
water industry charity, Water Aid. Its aim was to bring about
small-scale improvements in water supply and sanitation in the
developing world. North Surrey had been the first water company to
invite its customers to support Water Aid, by adding whatever they

felt like adding to their water bill when they paid the company. As a result, David and I began to build a friendship that survived long into our retirements.

We met for lunch at Great Fosters Hotel in Egham. David said to me, 'Générale des Eaux has heard all the talk about the possible privatisation of the regional water authorities and wants to be in a good position to know what is likely to happen. They've asked me to suggest some statutory water companies that it might be worth meeting. I've told them that if they were looking to invest in efficient companies, one of the best is North Surrey. What do you think about the possibility of linking with them?'

Sir Leonard Millis had died in July 1986 and Peter Davey had succeeded him as Chairman of the company. Although I had known Peter for some years as a non-executive director of North Surrey, Sutton and East Surrey water companies, I had not yet established the close understanding that I had with Sir Leonard, but I knew that I had to speak to Peter before doing anything other than saying to David, 'It could be a good idea but I'll have to talk to my Chairman before giving you an answer'. David replied, 'That's fine, and do pass on to him that Générale des Eaux has said that if you don't want to pursue the discussions, they'll go away'.

At that time the ordinary shares of statutory water companies were traded on the London Stock Exchange almost as the equivalent of Government gilt-edged stock because of the statutory limit on dividends that applied. Most of the ordinary shares in North Surrey paid a fixed dividend of three and a half per cent and at that time, traded at about thirty-five pence for a one-pound share. The company had issued about two million of these shares, which valued the company at something like two-thirds of a million pounds. Given that it had assets worth much more than that and a virtually guaranteed cash flow, the possibility of the removal of dividend limitations made the stock suddenly attractive to anyone with only a little imagination. If privatisation came about, there was likely to be a significant capital gain. If it didn't, the investment still produced a return of about ten per cent.

It surprised me that few UK investors seemed to understand what was happening. By the time of my meeting with David Kinnersley, a third French company, Saur, part of the Bouygues Group, had emerged as a player in addition to Générale des Eaux and Lyonnais.

Apart from these companies, the only other serious interest had come from an Australian investor called Duncan Saville. With no more to go on than what he read in his *Financial Times* in his office in Sydney, he recognised an opportunity and began to buy shares in a few water companies. He made a considerable profit. Some years later, he and I became colleagues on the Board of Directors of East Surrey Holdings plc.

Peter Davey and I met at his house just outside Guildford a few days after my lunch with David Kinnersley. Having told him the substance of what David had said, I went on, 'If the government goes ahead with privatisation, we can't be sure what will follow, but it seems clear that the statutory water companies will be under greater threat than at any time in the past. For instance, at North Surrey, we might well come under threat of take-over from a privatised Thames Water. If Thames took us over, I think that our works at Egham, Chertsey and Walton would continue as operational depots, but most of the management and administration of our company would go. Maybe half of the company's staff could lose their jobs.' Peter said, 'Wouldn't there be the same risk of job losses if we were taken over by Générale des Eaux?' I replied, 'There might be at some stage but not in the early years because they don't have an existing organisation in place all around North Surrey as does Thames.' Peter said, 'Well, Générale des Eaux could have bought shares without talking to us, so that may be a good sign of their fairness. Let's see what they have in mind.'

At about the same time, a letter arrived inviting Peter Davey and me to dinner in a private room at the Stafford Hotel in London to hear some ideas to be put forward on behalf of Cémentation-Saur. Cémentation was part of Trafalgar House, the large British company that was active in shipping and engineering. The boss of Trafalgar House was said to be friendly with the head of Bougyes in Paris and the combination of British and French engineering and French water experience seemed sensible to them. As a result, they had set up Cémentation-Saur as a joint venture to try to become involved in the privatisation of the water industry in England and Wales. At the dinner, Peter and I listened to the arguments put forward to persuade us to recognise Cémentation-Saur as an attractive suitor, and we could see much sense in what was said. However, at the end of the dinner, our host suddenly announced, 'By the way, you ought to know that we've bought ten per cent of North Surrey's shares this afternoon.' Peter said, 'Thank you for dinner. We'll get in touch.'

In the car on the way home, I asked Peter, 'What did you think of the evening?' He simply said, 'I didn't think much of them telling us at the end of the meeting that they'd already bought quite a lot of our stock without any consultation or discussion'. I was sufficiently familiar with Peter's understated style to know that any co-operation with Cémentation-Saur was highly unlikely.

By the autumn of 1987, with the agreement of the company, Générale des Eaux had bought almost twenty per cent of North Surrey stock. In September of that year there was a conference in Nice to mark the fortieth anniversary of the creation of the IWSA. Lady Millis was invited as the widow of one of the founders and Deborah and I escorted her to the meeting. Whilst in Nice, I was invited to have dinner with Jean-Pierre Tardieu at an excellent restaurant near the harbour. He put it to me that he hoped we would agree that the time was right for Générale des Eaux to take a more significant stake in North Surrey and I was able to tell him that my Chairman and my Board had no objection. By coincidence, sitting at a nearby table were two British delegates to the conference, Ken Roberts, the head of Wessex Water Authority and Eric Reed, a director of Thames Water. Both knew Jean-Pierre and both were personal friends of mine. There were knowing smiles from both when Jean-Pierre and I arrived and when we left!

A little later, it was agreed that Générale des Eaux would make a bid for the whole of the remaining shares in the company. It was an interesting experience for a Durham lad with no real business background. I had to recruit a firm of merchant bankers to advise the company and quickly had to learn what the issues were in such a negotiation as now began. Jean Claude Banon and I had several meetings to discuss the size of the offer to be made. The price of all statutory water company shares, including North Surrey, was now climbing rapidly as investors increasingly recognised the opportunity that they potentially offered. On behalf of his company, Jean Claude offered £7 per share, thus valuing North Surrey at about £14 million. Brown Shipley, our merchant bank, calculated that the price should be significantly more than that. The truth was that no one knew what a fair price would be because the water privatisation Bill was still in its Committee Stage.

This was a tricky situation. If the bid were agreed, the directors of North Surrey would have to write to the shareholders with a recommendation to sell at the agreed price with an endorsement from the company's merchant bankers. At a meeting with my Chairman, I said to Peter Davey, 'The trouble is that without knowledge of the final details of the regulatory system to be introduced, there isn't any way of knowing what the profitability of the company might be. That's why I don't want to push Générale des Eaux to a figure that could make it impossible for us to produce a reasonable return on their investment.' He saw the difficulty immediately and after long discussions, Peter and I agreed to ask our Board to recommend a bid of £8 per share.

Having agreed the bid with our Board, there were still difficult arguments to be won with Brown Shipley, who had little experience at that time of valuing regulated companies, even if the regulatory arrangements had been defined. Eventually, Brown Shipley came around, but soon after the letters to shareholders had gone out, the bank told me that a group of major shareholders wanted to meet me to discuss the offer. I arrived at the bank's offices in the City and when I entered the Boardroom, there was a group of about five or six people there. My recollection is that they all represented large insurance companies.

One of them was clearly accepted by the others as the unofficial leader and he began by saying, 'We're all unhappy about the offer that you and your Board is recommending. Our calculations vary, but none of us values North Surrey at less than £11 per share. Would you please tell us why you think that we should take your recommendation and accept £8 per share.' I replied, 'Let me turn the argument on its head and put it to you that had my Board decided to ask shareholders to reject the bid of £8, you would have asked for a similar meeting. But you'd have asked me why you shouldn't accept the bid and I wouldn't have been able to give you an answer. That's because the regulatory system hasn't been agreed so I couldn't calculate the costs of meeting new water quality and environmental regulation requirements and I don't know what the system of price controls will finally look like.'

There was a silence for ten or twenty seconds. It seemed longer, but eventually, the senior shareholder looked around at his colleagues and said, 'I think that's a fair answer. You're right. There is a lot of uncertainty about regulation and I'll be asking my people to agree to accept the offer of £8.' It was an enormous relief.

An agreed bid for Lee Valley Water Company, based at Hatfield, was announced at the same time as the North Surrey bid. Soon afterwards, Colne Valley Water Company was also taken over by Générale des Eaux. Their Chairman was Sir John Page who I knew well as my President at WCA. As a result of the take-over, at about that time, I suggested to Peter Davey that it might be a good idea for us to invite Jack Page to join the North Surrey Board. We invited Jack to join us for lunch and he agreed to join us on the Board at North Surrey.

The lunch was at Cliveden, the superb hotel overlooking the Thames just along the road from Jack's home at Taplow. Deborah and I had dinner there with Jack and Anne Page on a number of occasions. The first time the four of us dined there together, we met at Jack and Anne's house for a drink. Jack said to Deborah, 'Would you like a champagne cocktail?' to which she replied without hesitation, 'Oh, yes please'. That established Deborah in Jack's eyes as a woman to be reckoned with, a view that was cemented when she decided to refer to Cliveden as the 'Dog and Ferret'. It was the start of an enduring friendship.

Peter Davey had not been in the best of health for some time and in 1990, he decided to retire from the Board of North Surrey. He had been a good friend and a staunch ally through many difficult times in the Water Companies Association and during the take-over by Générale des Eaux. I could hardly have had better Chairmen than Leonard Millis and Peter Davey. To my surprise, Jean Claude Banon asked me to succeed Peter as Chairman of North Surrey whilst continuing as Managing Director. I combined the two roles from 1990 until July 1995, when I retired as Managing Director but continued as Chairman until North Surrey became part of Three Valleys Water in the autumn of 2000.

Eventually, Générale des Eaux took over six statutory water companies. They were: North Surrey, Lee Valley, Colne Valley (based at Watford), Rickmansworth and Uxbridge Valley, Folkestone and Tendring Hundred (based at Manningtree in Essex). Lee Valley, Rickmansworth and Colne Valley (where Sir John Page was Chairman) had been working together for some years. They had built and jointly operated (as Three Valleys Water Committee) a large water treatment plant at Iver, near Slough, so it was natural for Générale des Eaux to amalgamate the three companies as Three

Valleys Water plc. As they were in common ownership, the formal merger was straightforward, but there were long negotiations with the economic regulator, OFWAT, and a significant cut in the charges levied had to be agreed as the price of merging.

For some time, attention was focused on Three Valleys and the French holding company, General Utilities, was less involved with North Surrey, Folkestone and Tendring Hundred. The Chairman of Folkestone was (and still is in 2005) John Bonomy and the Chairman of Tendring Hundred was Jim Docwra, also a director of North Surrey.

Tendring Hundred had worked with Colchester Water Board in the sixties to build a reservoir at Ardleigh, near Colchester run by the Ardleigh Joint Committee. The Colchester Board had become part of Anglian Water Authority in 1974 and by 1990 Tendring was a partner at Ardleigh of Anglian Water plc. Through all the reorganisations in the water industry, the Committee had continued to work effectively, but tensions began to arise fairly soon after privatisation. New water quality requirements meant that there was a need for considerable capital expenditure. The two partners had different problems and there was to some extent a general reaction against the French companies by the big new regional water PLCs.

Differences began to be apparent between the Committee members on the right way to approach the problem and in 1992, Jean Claude Banon asked me if I would become a director of Tendring Hundred and become one of the Tendring members of the Ardleigh Committee. In 1995, I became Chairman of Tendring Hundred Water and an alternate Chairman of Ardleigh Committee.

Générale des Eaux had had a presence in the UK for a few years before water privatisation, having taken over a small former National Coal Board subsidiary, Associated Heat Services. This became the nucleus of the new British operation and a holding company, General Utilities Ltd, was set up. Offices were acquired in Headfort Place, not far from Belgrave Square in London and for several years, this became a second workplace for a group of us. Later, General Utilities moved to Old Queen Street and after Jean-Marie Messier became head of Générale des Eaux, he changed the name of the company to Vivendi.

Soon after, Messier split off the utility business as Vivendi Environnement, loading it with most of the group debt to allow him to borrow to buy various companies, including the US giant,

Universal. Thus, Générale des Eaux became Vivendi Universal and Vivendi Environnement while General Utilities became Vivendi UK. Someone wrote that a good indication of the time to sell shares in a company is when it changes its name and direction. That would certainly have been a good idea for those of us with shares in Vivendi Universal. But that is jumping ahead.

David Kinnersley had been asked to suggest a suitable Chairman for General Utilities. In his time at the National Water Council, he had worked under the chairmanship of Sir William Dugdale, and they had also been colleagues in the Association of River Authorities before the 1974 reorganisation. Sir William had been the first Chairman of Severn Trent Water Authority in 1974. He had retired from the National Water Council and given way to John Bellak as Chairman of Severn Trent but remained a great and well-respected figure in the water industry, so it was natural that David should suggest him to Jean Claude Banon.

Bill Dugdale was and is a larger than life character, usually ready to be politically incorrect. He'd won the MC in 1943, had a private pilot's licence (as did his wife, Cylla) and a plane at Coventry airport. He'd ridden in the Grand National, was a member of the Jockey Club and a Trustee of the Royal Shakespeare Company and had been Chairman of Aston Villa Football Club from 1973 to 1981. He became Chairman of General Utilities in 1989 and continued until 1999. He also joined my Board at North Surrey and became Chairman of Tendring Hundred Water, but in spite of all that, I never felt that his potential value to the group was fully recognised.

There were other interesting developments for me that flowed from the French connection. I was invited to join the Board of Compagnie des Eaux de Paris, the subsidiary of Générale des Eaux that supplies water to the part of Paris on the right bank of the Seine. I also joined the Board of the Générale des Eaux Research Company at Maison Lafitte, just outside Paris. There were many other meetings in France, usually in Paris and my French slowly improved a little, but it was always clear to me that my French colleagues understood my English much better than they did my French.

The poor quality of my French is well illustrated by one brief exchange in Paris. I had become a regular guest at the Hotel St Régis in Paris, a delightful small hotel in a quiet road near the Champs

Elysée. When I arrived on one of my visits, having practised in the taxi, I spoke to the receptionist in French. I felt quite pleased with myself until he replied in perfect English, 'Good evening Mr Jeffery. Do you still live in Curley Hill Road, Lightwater?'

Also in 1990, General Utilities decided to set up a company to provide engineering and scientific services to the water companies within the group. Jean Claude Banon asked me to be Chairman, and the new company was called General Utilities Projects Limited, quickly shortened to GUP.

Pascal Arnac came from Paris to be Managing Director and all except a small number of operational engineers and scientists in the group companies transferred to GUP. Jean Claude wanted GUP to become a show-place 'centre of excellence'. General Utilities Ltd was the British face of Générale des Eaux and he was keen to show that his company was a major player. It was easy to understand this ambition from the General Utilities' perspective. On the other hand, I felt I had to tell Jean Claude that there was a risk that if we created an élite group of strategic planners, it might lead to the operational managers gradually becoming seen in a sense as second-rate.

I said, 'Many of the problems that I've met in the past have had their roots in the hierarchy that places planning engineers and consultant engineers above operational staff. So often, schemes are designed without proper involvement of the people who later have to make them work. The difficulties that frequently arise during and after commissioning could usually have been avoided if the operational people had been properly brought into the planning process. I've worked hard to have the importance of operational managers recognised and we must make sure that the creation of a centre of excellence doesn't undermine that.'

That point is just one example of the general difficulty of getting the balance right between centralisation and delegation. Although Jean Claude accepted the principle, and GUP did a great deal of excellent work, I'm not sure that we were as successful as we ought to have been in getting that balance right.

The price review of the water industry by OFWAT in 1999 signalled the end of my career in the water industry. It resulted in large reductions in charges to apply from April 2000, and the companies in our group were fairly typical in facing a reduction in income of between 15% and 17%. As a result, it was decided that

North Surrey should be taken over by Three Valleys Water and that Tendring Hundred and Folkestone should make economies by sharing services. I was invited to join the Board of Three Valleys as Deputy Chairman for one year, joining in the autumn of 2000 and retiring at the end of September 2001. I stood down as Chairman of Tendring Hundred in 2000, remaining as a director and member of the Ardleigh Joint Committee until I finally retired at the end of December 2002.

Although a part of me will always think of North Surrey as 'my company', I know that such feelings are irrational. Nevertheless, it was sad to see a company that had been based in Egham for almost 120 years disappear and to have to say goodbye to many friends as well as colleagues. And leaving Tendring Hundred and Ardleigh was also a little sad. I'd enjoyed helping Tendring Hundred to retain a degree of independence, and working to build a good relationship with Anglian Water colleagues on the Ardleigh Committee.

I'd also enjoyed staying at the Pier Hotel at Harwich the night before meetings and the fish and chips in the excellent restaurant there, first with Bill Dugdale and John Rayner, the Managing Director of Tendring Hundred. Then, after Bill Dugdale retired from the Tendring Board, the dinners continued with John Rayner and my eventual replacement as Chairman, Peter Darby. In ten years on the Board, I had made some good friends and had developed a respect for the part that the company played in the local community. Two examples of this were the support given by the company to the Essex University Choir and its annual concert in Colchester, and the strong link with the Tendring Show, of which John Rayner was President in 1999.

My years in the water industry after privatisation and the French take-over of North Surrey were in many ways the most satisfying of my career. I was given a wider brief than would otherwise have been possible and was made to feel valued. In 1995, when I retired as Managing Director of North Surrey, I was given a farewell dinner in the Beaufort Room at the Savoy Hotel in London. Between thirty and forty colleagues and friends attended, including Bill and Cylla Dugdale, Jack and Anne Page and Jean Claude and Ana Banon. Jean Claude made a speech that was full of praise for my work and Jack Page recited a poem that he had written for the evening. At the end of his speech, Jean Claude said, 'We all know that Jack loves wine, especially the red wines from Bordeaux. Jack joined the water industry in 1961 and as that was an outstanding year for Bordeaux reds, we've a bottle of Chateau Palmer 1961 and some wine glasses from Tiffany's for him to mark his retirement.'

All that would have been more than enough to make the evening special, but after the main course, Jean Claude stood up and said, 'We all know how much Jack and Deborah love music, so we've arranged a surprise.' The curtain along the stage that sits at the side of the Beaufort Room was drawn back to reveal eight members of the London Mozart Players, who then played the Schubert Octet. It was a truly wonderful experience.

I've been so lucky in my working relationships and in contriving to maintain an active role in the water industry until near the end of my seventy-third year. Apart from my friends and work at North Surrey and in the Water Companies Association, I've been able to travel all over the world, from Canada to Australia, from Brazil and Argentina to Japan, South Africa, the Philippines and Malaysia. Perhaps my strongest and most lasting impression is that everywhere I've been and whatever the system under which water services are provided, I've found the same friendship and dedication among the men and women who make the system work for the health and well-being of society.

It's Joy at the Savoy
19 July 1995

When Jack was just a little boy
he filled his parents' hearts with joy.
This sturdy, active, brainy child,
who never cried and always smiled
and never sought to break a rule,
became the idol of his school.

He always knew how words were spelled,
at chemistry he quite excelled –
with French he really had to stick it
but best of all he loved his cricket.
He chided youngsters who were naughty
and played with verve the piano forte.
His books he loved – an avid reader –
in all his groups he was the leader.

As years roll by, behold the truth –
the Man is mirror of the Youth,
and these fine qualities expand
to take new challenges in hand.

With loved North Surrey as his base
his reputation grows apace –
exciting jobs grew quite irrationally
at home and internationally.
(I cannot rhyme all those initials
of where Jack's one of their officials).

So why is Jack so keenly sought?
We really think the answer ought
to be that his experience,
wide knowledge, drive and common sense
is what they need to run the show.
But actually, we really know
the reason why is it's all begun –
Because Jack's such tremendous fun!

Beside him over all these years,
with far more happiness than tears
to help him in his busy life
stands Deborah, his loving wife,
who's always there his hand to press
or drive him in her XJS.
His mother too is there applauding,
she finds his triumphs so rewarding.

Is there another who aspires
to praise this chap who she admires?
Ah! yes – the Queen's a fan you see
by making him a CBE.
A final touch to mark our joy
this happy night at the Savoy.

Jack Page

CHAPTER 10

The US of A and all that jazz

America is so vast that almost everything said about it is likely to be true, and the opposite is probably equally true

James T Farrell, Introduction to H L Mencken's
Prejudices: A Selection (1958)

A S A SMALL BOY before the war, I spent a lot of time reading and looking at reference books such as *Wonders of the World*. Many of these my father had bought at so much per week from Odhams Press, the publisher of the *Daily Herald*, which was the Labour Party newspaper. These books introduced me to images of natural wonders like Victoria Falls as well as to man-made wonders like the skyscrapers of Manhattan in New York. Talking pictures that had appeared at the end of the twenties reinforced the stimulation through the 'travelogues' (So, as the sun sinks slowly in the west, we say, 'farewell' to the wherever) that were commonly shown in the cinemas of the thirties as support for the main feature. And a good proportion of the films we saw as children were set in New York, including series such as 'The Dead End Kids' and many feature films.

When all of this was added to my growing interest in jazz, it made the United States a very exciting prospect. Jazz had its roots in New Orleans, moving up the Mississippi through Kansas City to Chicago in the twenties and thirties and then becoming established in New York. By the time the war ended in 1945, I had graduated in jazz terms from the music of the Original Dixieland Jazz Band and Bob Crosby to what we began to call modern jazz. The music being pioneered by black American musicians like Charlie Parker and Dizzy Gillespie became known as bebop and was more exciting than any music I'd heard before.

I also recognised a social context that matched my strong feelings about racial intolerance and my awareness of the horrors of the Klu Klux Klan, epitomised by the great Billie Holliday recording of 'Strange Fruit'. Many of us thought that, being aware of how much of earlier jazz had been plagiarised and commercialised by white bands, the beboppers were setting out to create a new kind of music that only a minority would understand. To some extent they drew on developments in European music, using much more complex harmonies than those of the traditional blues, coupled with a departure from the typically steady four in a bar rhythms of the past.

So from my teenage years, the United States and especially New York had a special significance for me. When the opportunity came to visit New York for the IWSA Congress in 1972, it was something that had seemed an impossible dream for thirty years. Our plane landed at JFK airport on Long Island on a warm September afternoon and I still recall the excitement of my first glimpse of the Chrysler Building as we approached Manhattan. As soon as I'd checked in at the Hilton Hotel, I set out to explore. The hotel was only a block from 52nd Street, home of all the jazz clubs of the forties, so that was my first stop, but sadly the old clubs had closed long ago.

Then I found a cinema museum showing a series of the short films that had been made in the forties featuring big bands, but that wasn't quite what I'd hoped to find. Later in the week I heard more live jazz, including the Bill Evans trio in Greenwich Village and Roy Eldridge at Jimmy Ryan's just around the corner from the Hilton, but I really didn't have much spare time on that first visit.

For a few years, it seemed that that would be the limit of my experience of the USA. Then, soon after I was appointed General Manager of North Surrey in 1977, I had a call from my friend Tom Palin at Newcastle and Gateshead Water Company. He said, 'There's a water quality conference organised by the AWWA (American Waterworks Association) at Kansas City in December. I'm going, so why don't you suggest to Leonard Millis that you ought to go too?' When he had appointed me as General Manager, my Chairman, Leonard Millis had said to me, 'The water industry is going to change a lot in the next few years. You should become a good manager but you'd be wise to keep up your involvement in water quality as well.' Therefore, I thought that I might get a good response to my request and I was right.

Tom and I flew to Kansas City via New York and arranged to break our journey on the way home for a few days in New York. We had a great time and I began to get to know a few people in the AWWA. Over the next twenty years or so, I was fortunate to make a number of good friends in AWWA, people like Jack Mannion, long-time Director of AWWA and Jerry Gilbert, a Past President of AWWA and once boss of East Bay MUD (Metropolitan Utilities Districts), the organisation that supplies water services to Oakland, across the bay from San Francisco.

My assimilation into the US water industry was made easier by the links that were growing between AWWA and IWSA. One of my old colleagues in the UK water industry was Len Bays. He had been Chemist at Bristol Waterworks Company before becoming Distribution Manager there. Len became a great personal friend. He is a Yorkshireman and I've sometimes reminded him of the old saying, 'You can always tell a Yorkshireman, – but you can't tell him much'. Len played league football for Hull City and was a larger than life character, much respected in the water industry in the UK and abroad. He became Secretary General of the IWSA in the early eighties and began to include me in various IWSA activities. For example, I was invited to participate in two or three joint IWSA/ AWWA workshops. One of these was held in Toronto in 1990, just before the Annual AWWA Conference, held that year in Cincinnati, Ohio.

Some relatives of my mother had emigrated from the north-east of England to Canada in the twenties and lived in Ontario, some in Toronto and some in Peterborough, not too far along the lake. I said to my mother, 'Would you like to go to Toronto with Deborah and me and look up one or two of your relatives?' I half expected her to refuse because she was eighty-five years old at the time and had never taken a flight of that duration, but she just said, 'That sounds lovely. When are we going?' So my mother flew from Newcastle to Heathrow, as she'd done quite often to visit us after my father died. The three of us then flew to Toronto on a British Airways 747. I told a steward that this was my mother's first ever flight outside the UK and as we approached Toronto, he gave my mother a bottle of champagne to mark the occasion. My mother thanked him and then said, 'I must give you a kiss' and promptly did so, somewhat to his surprise, I think.

We stayed at the Four Seasons Hotel in Toronto for the four days of the workshop and Mother charmed everyone at the various social events. One day, Deborah arranged for a chauffeur to drive them to Niagara in a limousine and my mother so much enjoyed travelling in style to see Niagara Falls. Many of her Canadian relatives lived in

Author with his mother, CNN Tower, Toronto, 1990

Peterborough in Ontario and after the workshop, the son of her cousin collected my mother and took her to meet the family while Deborah and I flew to Cincinnati for the AWWA meeting. After the conference there, we had a few days in Peterborough before bringing my mother back to the UK. She had a lot to tell her friends in Tanfield Lea when she got home after her first and only trip abroad.

When Deborah and I married in 1983, we were able to combine our honeymoon touring the United States with attendance at the Annual AWWA Conference taking place in Las Vegas, Nevada a few weeks after our wedding. There were just a few close friends at our wedding breakfast at Great Fosters Hotel in Egham on 28 May. My mother and Deborah's mother, Evelyn were there with our friends Gillian and Alan Mason, Dick and Nina Faulkner and Barrie and Diana Allcock. Alan and Dick were cricketing friends, and Barrie and I had been members of Egham Round Table in our thirties. At the end of the party, Barrie put on a peaked cap and drove us to Heathrow to catch our 7 p.m. Pan Am flight to JFK, New York and back to the New York Hilton where we'd met in 1972.

On Monday, 30 May, we took a taxi from the Hilton to La Guardia airport for our flight to San Francisco. We'd booked a hire car to get from San Francisco to Las Vegas and at La Guardia airport, I said to Deborah, 'You did pack my driving licence, didn't you?' Even after more than twenty years, I still can't bring myself to repeat her response, but I did need my licence. So as soon as we reached the Four Seasons Clift in San Francisco (by which time it was approaching midnight in Lightwater), I called our neighbour, 'Mickey' Rooney and explained the problem. Mickey and Pam had a key to the house in Lightwater to which we'd moved from Camberley in 1979 and I described to Mickey exactly where he'd find the licence.

Mickey had been a British Airways pilot before ill health forced him to stop flying, and by that time he had become a flying instructor for BA. Mickey said, 'I may be able to get it on tomorrow's flight. Give me a call tomorrow afternoon, UK time.' I suggested that if he were able to persuade someone to carry the licence, it might be simplest if they left the licence at the British Airways desk at San Francisco airport. Mickey ignored that and replied, 'Just give me a call tomorrow and I'll be able to tell you whether I've been able to do anything'. So at about 8 a.m. in San Francisco and 4 p.m. in Surrey on Tuesday, I phoned Mickey again.

He told me, 'Your driving licence left Heathrow for San Francisco about three hours ago. They thought it was a bit dangerous to leave it at the BA desk because of shift changes and asked you to pick it up from them at their hotel.' 'Thanks for solving everything, Mickey. What's the name of their hotel? 'The Four Seasons Clift.' 'I can't believe it. That's where we're staying.' 'Well, you'll be able to buy them a drink then.'

So that afternoon, Deborah and I waited in the lobby of the Clift. When three men in BA uniform arrived at about 5 p.m., I introduced myself to one of them. He confirmed that they did indeed have my licence and I asked them if they'd like to join Deborah and me for a drink. 'Give us twenty minutes to have a shower and we'll see you in the bar.' So it came about that three hours later, after too many Manhattans, Deborah and I had a slight struggle to walk in a straight line in making our way to the restaurant. The crew were great fun and had assumed that I must be a director of BA to have been able to persuade the company to answer my emergency call.

Deborah and I really enjoyed our few days at the Clift in the beautiful city of San Francisco. We crossed the Bay to Sausalito, saw

Alcatraz from the ferry, had dinner in Chinatown and walked and walked.

Having picked up our hire car in San Francisco, we drove to Monterey, a place I knew slightly from a previous visit a couple of years earlier and that I felt I knew well from reading Steinbeck's *Cannery Row* and his wonderful book, *The Log from the Sea of Cortez*. We dined at the Sardine Factory and had a great time, before driving across California to Yosemite to stay at a hotel just outside the village in the heart of the National Park. It was called the Wawona Inn and the BA pilot who had brought my driving licence to San Francisco had recommended it. It consisted of several wooden buildings in a truly magnificent setting with bears wandering around nearby and it was wonderful.

After a couple of days there, we drove south to Fresno. When we unpacked at the Holiday Inn there, I realised that I'd left behind a pair of trousers at the Wawona Inn. At dinner, I mentioned to our waitress that my wife had forgotten to pack my trousers when we left Yosemite. She looked at me in some amazement and said, 'Your wife forgot to pack *YOUR* trousers!' To have forgotten my driving licence and my trousers and to have blamed my wife each time within a week of our marriage was not a good start!

The next morning, we returned to Yosemite and collected the said trousers before setting off for Bairstow, famous to me as one of the list of towns in the lyric of Nat King Cole's 'Route 66'. From there, we drove across the desert to Las Vegas. I'd been there in 1980 with Roger Gardiner, who had joined North Surrey from Bristol Waterworks as Chemist. We had had a weekend there before going on to Colorado Springs for a water quality conference, including a flight over the Grand Canyon. It was somewhat different to be in Vegas as part of the huge AWWA Annual Conference. We stayed in the Hilton Hotel, where the Conference was based and where Roger and I had stayed in 1980. Quite a number of colleagues from the UK water industry were also there.

On one evening, Deborah and I went with Eric Reed and his wife, Joan, to hear Keely Smith singing in cabaret at The Dunes. She had made some great records in the fifties with the wild band of Louis Prima that often played at Las Vegas then, but on this occasion she sang some ballads in a more restrained style. At that time, Eric was Head of Operations at Thames Water Authority. He'd served in the

RAF as a fighter pilot in the Battle of Britain and had been awarded the DFC. Eric had a droll sense of humour and in the taxi to The Dunes, engaged the taxi driver in a slightly bizarre conversation about the vocal group from the forties called the Ink Spots. I'm pretty sure that the young driver had never heard of the group but nothing would deter Eric once he'd started.

At the end of the Conference, we flew from Las Vegas to New Orleans and checked into the Royal Hotel. We had a wonderful few days there in what had been the cradle of jazz in the early part of the twentieth century. We had dinner at Antoine's, Sunday brunch alfresco with a jazz group playing at the Court of Two Sisters, and Eggs Benedict for breakfast at Brennan's as well as exploring Bourbon Street, Jackson Square etc. In Jackson Square, a young painter did a portrait of Deborah in crayons that now hangs in our library at Hedley. Then we flew back to Heathrow via New York after a fantastic trip.

When my eldest daughter, Wyn, approached the milestone of her fortieth birthday, Deborah and I asked her if she and her husband, Gareth, would like to celebrate her birthday in New York. It took less than a second for her to say, 'Yes', and so at the end of March 1991, the four of us embarked on a Virgin Airways flight from Gatwick to Newark New Jersey. There was a mix-up when we arrived at Gatwick, the details of which I can no longer remember, but I do remember being quite cross at the time.

Whatever the problem, the outcome was that we were offered an upgrade to upper class. However, there was a new difficulty at that stage when the clerk spotted that Gareth was wearing jeans. She said, 'I'm sorry, but I can't upgrade anyone wearing jeans.' It was not the time to question the logic of the policy so I replied, 'Don't worry, he'll have a new pair of trousers before we board.' Gareth and I then rushed into the Burton's shop at the airport and bought the one pair of conventional trousers in the shop that Gareth was prepared to wear and travelled to Newark in comfort.

The four of us had a splendid holiday in what could be described as changeable weather. There was snow on the day after we arrived and the temperature was high enough for sunbathing on the next day. We had dinner with our friend Judy Gilbert, wife of Jerry, who happened to be in New York from California for a meeting with the publisher of her books on English as a second language. We also did the Circle Line tour around Manhattan Island that Deborah and I had first done in 1972 and we had dinner in the Rainbow Room. Coincidentally, the star of the cabaret that night was Keely Smith who we'd seen at The Dunes in Las Vegas in 1983 with Eric and Joan Reed.

I attended AWWA meetings regularly and as a result, saw quite a lot of the major cities, including Kansas City on two occasions. My first trip there was with Tom Palin in December 1977, when it was as cold as anywhere I've ever visited. The second time was in June and as my taxi left the airport, I saw a temperature display showing a hundred and eight degrees Fahrenheit. There can't be many places with such extremes of temperature.

My growing involvement with AWWA led to several invitations to present papers to AWWA meetings. As I've mentioned, in the autumn of 1992 I gave a paper on UK water quality regulation at a meeting of the AWWA water quality group in Toronto.

Then, in the summer of 1993, I gave a paper on water privatisation in England and Wales at the Annual Conference of AWWA in San Antonio, Texas. The American water supply industry was predominantly run by municipalities but there was growing interest in water privatisation at that time, and the whole economic and environmental regulatory package that had been developed in England and Wales. The US water industry is essentially conservative and resistant to change but there was considerable interest, the meeting room was packed and there was a lively discussion. Afterwards, Deborah and I had a total change of tack when we visited the Alamo Museum. Somehow, the museum managed to give an impression of the Alamo that was at the same time smaller and yet more impressive than the image presented in the sixties' Hollywood film.

In 1994, Deborah and I returned once more to the United States and the New York Hilton for the AWWA Annual Conference. This was a special occasion for me, because I was presented with Honorary Membership of the American Waterworks Association at the opening ceremony of the Conference. This is an honour that is not often conferred on people from outside the United States and I joined a fairly small group from the UK that includes my old friend from IWSA, Len Bays, and Michael Rouse, once of WRc and later Chief Drinking Water Inspector.

The 1995 AWWA Conference was held in June at Anaheim near Los Angeles and was my last before retirement as Managing Director of North Surrey. Deborah and I were guests at the President's Dinner on the Sunday evening and we had no time to spare because our flight from London did not land at Los Angeles until the late afternoon on that day. When we got to our hotel, it was almost time for the dinner and so we were the last of the guests to arrive. Someone had told the AWWA President that it had been announced on the previous day that I had been appointed CBE and when we walked in, there was a round of applause. Photographs were taken of us with the AWWA President. The warmth everyone showed to us was amazing. It was a moving moment and a generous gesture by our American friends.

At the end of the conference, during which I had been quite poorly with a chest infection, Deborah and I drove a rented car to Palm Springs for a few days' rest. While there, we went to dinner at a Thai restaurant near our hotel and there was Keely Smith again, this time having a meal at the next table. Having heard her sing in Las

Investiture at Buckingham Palace, 1995

Vegas and in New York, I still regret not having the courage to say 'Hello'.

After Palm Springs, we drove to Long Beach and took the ferry to beautiful Santa Catalina Island. We loved being there and saw bison, as well as visiting the Avalon ballroom, where the great bands of Benny Goodman, Stan Kenton and others had played in the thirties and forties. It was wonderfully nostalgic.

There were many other trips to New York, because even when the US conference I was attending was elsewhere in the States, I usually managed to arrange to fly via New York. The AWWA Annual Conference was in Dallas in June 1998 and I visited the museum from where Lee Harvey Oswald is believed to have shot President John Kennedy in November 1963. On the way home, I had two nights in the Algonquin Hotel in New York. On the first evening, I went to Carnegie Hall and saw a double bill featuring Diana Krall and George Shearing. The next night, I had dinner in the Oak Room at the Algonquin and heard a truly memorable cabaret performance by one of my favourite singers, Susannah McCorkle. She was in great form in a programme that was a tribute to George Gershwin and I was able to speak to her briefly and have her autograph the sleeve of one of her CDs afterwards. It was an enormous shock to me to hear of her suicide just a year or so later.

Another US visit was to Seattle in November 1997 to take part in a seminar on efficiency in the water industry jointly organised by the American Waterworks Association and the Seattle Water Department. The seminar was organised by my old AWWA friend Jerry Gilbert from Orinda across the Bay from San Francisco, and Diana Gale. Diana ran Seattle Public Utilities ably assisted by Paul Reiter as Director of Strategic Policy. Jerry had introduced me to Diana at meetings of IWSA and AWWA and they invited me to kick off the seminar in a debate on privatisation with Jerry. Jerry and I stood at lecterns at either side of the platform in a kind of model of the US televised presidential debates.

Jerry said that many in the United States worried about introducing privatisation into the water industry because of the fundamental importance of water to society and the risks that society associates with privatisation. I said, 'I can't understand why so many people in the US water industry are so opposed to privatisation when the culture of the United States is so dominated by private enterprise.

Many of us took the risk of flying to this meeting in Seattle, the home of Mr Boeing who built so many of those airplanes that brought us here. Presumably we all think that flying in a plane built by the private sector is a reasonable thing to do so why are you so worried about the private sector in water?' Jerry replied, 'Water's different.'

My last visit to New York was in May 2001 when I was part of a UK delegation to the meeting of the United Nations Commission on Sustainable Development, through my involvement with the World Humanity Action Trust, of which I shall say a little more later. I also visited the United States twice in 2005, the first time to attend a meeting of the Executive Committee of the International Humanist and Ethical Union (of which, again, more later) in Martha's Vineyard, south of Boston.

Then on 27 October of the same year, Deborah and I flew to Miami to join a jazz cruise at Fort Lauderdale. We landed just three days after Hurricane Wilma had struck. The hotel in Fort Lauderdale where we'd reserved a room was closed and the hotel in Miami where we ended up had itself been closed for twenty-four hours

Family group at The Savoy after the Investiture, left to right, Wyn, Deborah, Gareth, the author, Darole, Andy and Jill

because of the lack of power. Our journey from Miami airport to the hotel was eerie because most of the traffic lights and street lighting were not working and there were few people about because a curfew was in operation. When we left Florida on 5 November we were told that over one million people were still without power.

Coming so soon after the inundation of most of New Orleans following an earlier hurricane it began to make more people in the United States and elsewhere think that maybe there is something in the concerns some of us have been expressing about the unsustainable nature of our society and the dangers of climate change.

CHAPTER 11

Clubbable

The secret of success in society is a certain heartiness and sympathy.

R W Emerson, *Essays, Second Series*, 1844

UNLIKE GROUCHO MARX, who famously said, 'I don't want to belong to any club that will accept me as a member' I suppose I'm what Leonard Millis used to describe as 'clubbable'. In 1960, I joined an investment club of cricketers from Chester-le-Street Cricket Club; I joined Egham Round Table in the mid-sixties and then became a member of Ashford Rotary Club. My general wish to 'belong' was probably partly a result of my feelings of isolation over politics and religion when I was a schoolboy and the insecurity that that created in me. The one exception was my reaction to a suggestion that I should become a Freemason.

At Christmas time 1961, soon after our move from Chester-le-Street to Middlesex, my eldest daughter, Wyn, was invited to a party at a friend's house. I went to pick her up afterwards and was invited by the father of her friend to have a coffee. It emerged that we both worked in the water industry, he being employed by the Metropolitan Water Board. We'd not been chatting for long when he said to me, 'If you want to get on in the water industry, you ought to join my lodge.' I thanked him for the advice, but on the way home, I thought, 'I couldn't deal with not knowing whether anything I might achieve in my career was due to my own efforts and ability or to my being a Freemason.' I never followed it up although gradually, I came to know that many of my colleagues were Masons.

In the mid-sixties, a new Rotary Club was set up in Egham and the Chief Engineer and his Deputy at South West Suburban Water Company, Jack Brock-Griggs and Gordon Hicks joined. Shortly afterwards, Egham Round Table was established as a sort of Rotary for the under-forties and I was invited to become a member. I joined and for a few years enjoyed getting to know a varied group of young men with a different range of interests from my scientific and engineering background. They included a dentist, a local bank manager, a lawyer, an estate agent, a sign writer and men from several other professions and occupations.

In time, I realised that many Rotarians and Round Tablers were Freemasons, although at the same time, many are also strongly opposed to Freemasonry. To me, the main difference was that Rotary and Round Table were open organisations and members advertised their membership by wearing their badges. I saw a comparison with the fact that conflicts of interest in politics and business have far less significance after they've been openly declared.

Round Table meetings were usually chaotic and the highlight was often the mumbled and hilarious reading by our secretary, Jim Donaldson, of the minutes of the previous meeting, with frequent interruptions from members.

When I became Chairman of Egham Round Table, the induction evening was informal to say the least. As I worked in the water industry, those planning the evening decided that it would be fun to have water as a theme. A 'throne' was built for me consisting of a WC seat and throughout the dinner, a tape recording of a WC flushing was played. Unfortunately, the liquid refreshment that was organised was not a success. Knowing that I brewed my own beer at that time, the organisers raided my garage and brought my brew to the dinner. Sadly, they picked it up only a few hours before the dinner and the beer was a long way from settling after being shaken up in someone's car. It had an absolutely foul taste and was poured down the drain.

Life in Round Table was enjoyable and relaxing, but there was also a strong element of community service mixed with the fun. For example, for several years, we joined with other Round Tables in the area working with Bentall's store in Kingston to take people suggested by the local social services department in our cars to the late-night shopping at Christmas time. We also stripped down an ancient Austin Somerset car and replaced the body with a brightly painted replica steam locomotive that we called the Runnymede Rocket. For some years, rides on the Rocket were very popular with children at our Round Table Gala and at local occasions such as the Egham Show.

A year or so after joining Egham Round Table, I joined Ashford Rotary Club. The average age there was considerably higher than in Round Table but the basic approach was similar. We enjoyed our

lunches and our social functions but there was also a strong emphasis
on community service. A speaker at one of our lunches was from the
probation service and he invited members to consider becoming a
Voluntary Associate Probation Officer. I and two other members
were accepted and I was asked to help a young man who was on
probation for setting fire to his landlady's car. I think I was chosen
because the man came from County Durham and it was thought that
it might be easier for me to build some kind of relationship with him.

His story, verified by his Probation Officer, was a sad one and it
was clear that the odds had been stacked against him from an early
age. I helped him find a job and another place to live and for a time,
I felt things were going quite well. But after about three months, he
turned up one Friday afternoon at my office and asked me if I could
cash a cheque for him. He'd given up his job and had decided to
move to Manchester. As he had no bank account, he needed to
convert his pay cheque into cash to buy a train ticket, so I cashed the
cheque for him. He thanked me and I never saw him again.

The experience taught me to appreciate the work done by
probation officers. They are sometimes criticised but in my short
experience, I found them to be understanding but never naïve and
I'm sure there are many thousands of offenders all over the country
who are helped to re-build a place in our society through their
efforts.

There were only about thirty members of Ashford Rotary Club at
that time and perhaps this helped us to be able to respond quickly in
an emergency. In the spring of 1970, there was a severe earthquake
at Gediz in Turkey. It was clear from the start that there was
widespread devastation. The Club President supported the idea of
Ashford Rotary sponsoring a national Rotary appeal for money to
provide emergency support, and four of us agreed to go to Turkey.

Within a few days, we had raised well over one thousand pounds
and bought a caravan, blankets, tinned food, etc. The Ford Motor
Company agreed to lend us a car to tow the caravan to Turkey, we
were offered free petrol in the UK and we obtained the necessary
documentation from the Turkish Embassy. Within a week of the
earthquake, we were on our way.

We left Ashford at lunchtime on a Friday. As far as I can
remember, none of us had towed a caravan before and we came close
to disaster on the journey to Dover. I was driving down the hill

towards the Medway at about sixty miles per hour when the caravan
was hit suddenly by a crosswind. It began to sway quite violently
from side to side. It was tempting to brake but I knew that that was
likely to add to the risk so I just took my foot off the throttle and
allowed the combination to slow naturally. It was a great relief when
the swaying gradually reduced and we were able to continue
normally. Of course, there was then a sustained period of assessment
of my driving ability, or rather of my lack of it, by my three
colleagues.

After crossing the Channel, we stopped for dinner not far outside
Calais. One member of the group, John Fader, had dual British and
Swiss nationality and was convinced that Swiss francs were universally
acceptable. The Swiss reputation for financial acumen had led us to
accept him as our expert on money matters before our departure.
However, that acceptance was soon challenged. After dinner, John
asked for the bill and attempted to pay with his Swiss francs. Of
course, they were refused. None of us had any French francs but
fortunately I'd just acquired my first credit card and that was
accepted.

After dinner, we set off towards Germany, sharing the driving.
Soon after dawn, somewhere near Aachen, we stopped at a rest area
for a few hours' sleep and then set off again. We spent Saturday night
in a small hotel in Salzburg and drove on to reach Zagreb on Sunday.
From Zagreb, we travelled south on Monday on the Yugoslav
motorway towards Bulgaria. Although called a motorway, the road
was not good at that time. It was single-carriageway and some skill
was required to negotiate the many potholes. After towing the
caravan through Belgrade, also an interesting experience, we entered
Bulgaria and headed for Sofia, where we stayed on Monday night.
The hotel was fairly new and the rooms had bathrooms but the
plumbing would certainly not have complied with British water
by-laws. On Tuesday, we drove through Nis and Plovdiv and
through mile after mile of orchards, eventually reaching the Turkish
border near Edirne. In Nis, we saw a man with a dancing bear,
something I had never expected to see and something I hope never
to see again.

Up to this point, we had had no problems at customs checks, but
that changed at Edirne. Customs officers refused to believe that this
group of Englishmen would be mad enough to drive from England

to Turkey to give away a caravan and all its contents. We had a letter from the Turkish Embassy and had attached notices in Turkish to the outside of the caravan saying who we were and what we were doing, but they were not convinced. They searched everywhere, including under the bonnet of the car and under the car and the caravan while we waited anxiously. Eventually, after between two and three hours, they were satisfied and suddenly became friendly.

The boss spoke English and he asked us, 'Have you booked a hotel in Istanbul?' We replied that we hadn't arranged anything and he said, 'My sister has a very nice hotel. It is very cheap and she will look after you very well.'

It sounded like a good idea, so we took the card he gave us with the address of the hotel and drove off. We reached Istanbul in the rush hour and found the square we were looking for. The square was a complete free-for-all with absolutely no evidence of traffic rules. Somehow, we found the hotel, parked the car and caravan and went in. We explained that the brother of the owner had sent us there. The owner appeared and welcomed us and showed us to our rooms. Mine was clean and seemed OK for two or three days. After a wash, we went downstairs and entered what we imagined was the lounge. There were ten or twelve attractive young women sitting around the room and it quickly became clear even to a group of innocent English Rotarians that this was not a typical English hotel. We attempted to look suave and sophisticated and sat down, but soon we had to leave and share our impressions of the place in which we'd found ourselves, accompanied by a fair amount of giggling.

On the next day, we visited the Turkish Red Crescent and arranged to hand over the caravan and its contents. We saw enough of Istanbul in the next day or so to realise what an intriguing place it is, where Europe meets Asia, and the mix of cultures is fascinating. We saw the Blue Mosque and the Sea of Marmara and rode in one or two of the shared taxis that were a feature of Istanbul but once again, John Fader's financial skills let us down. There was some confusion over exchange rates involving, as I recall, special tourist rates. John was convinced that he had worked out a way in which we could exploit the system and make money but needless to say, when we followed his advice, all of us lost money!

I don't suppose that our efforts were significant in the context of the scale of the disaster at Gediz but at least we made a gesture of support and showed that we cared. We certainly learned a great deal from the trip. It was a wonderful experience.

In the late seventies, when Sir Leonard Millis was Master of the Plumbers Company, he invited Deborah and me to be his guests at a Worshipful Company of Plumbers' dinner. I was flattered and pleased by this confirmation that Deborah and I were now accepted as a couple after some difficult years. Other invitations to Plumbers' events followed and one day, Leonard asked me if I'd like to become a Plumber. My private reaction to the invitation was somewhat complicated.

I'd seen the invitation coming and part of me was pleased but part of me wondered whether by accepting, I'd be selling out the principles that had been important to me since childhood. In particular, as the motto of the Company is 'In God is All Our Hope', I was worried that there might be an overtly religious content to the admission ceremony, but a few discrete enquiries assured me that there wasn't.

Author, Master of the Plumbers Company, and his wife, 1996

I read up a little about the Company and found that 'The Company exists to:

(a) Foster, maintain and develop links with all aspects of plumbing, including gas, sewage and water industries.
(b) Promote as appropriate youth activities in the craft by financial and technical contributions to educational and vocational ventures.
(c) Contribute to Charity through the Company's Charitable and Educational Trust, which provides grants to improve the educational and management aspects of plumbing, as well as grants to the City of London charities.
(d) Support the 'Pursuit of Excellence' so that through contact with other organisations the Company is able to call on past experience for the benefit of future enterprises.
(e) Provide a pleasant social ambience for those in the Company.'

I felt happy with all of these objectives and came to the somewhat self-righteous and pompous conclusion that as I was happy with the objectives, liked the Plumbers I'd met, and as the Plumbers Company was not a secret society it would be churlish to reject Leonard's suggestion. So I applied to become a Plumber. My application was proposed by Past Master Sir Leonard Millis and seconded by Past Master Barron Holroyd, a non-executive director of North Surrey Water Company.

Having become a Freeman of the Plumbers Company, the next step in the process of joining was to apply for the Freedom of the City of London and I was admitted to the Freedom of the City of London on 25 November 1980 at a simple ceremony in the Guildhall in the City of London. Shortly afterwards, I became a Liveryman of the Worshipful Company of Plumbers of London at a meeting of the Court in Carpenters Hall. The Master who admitted me was David Thomson, a man descended from two winners of the Nobel Prize for Physics.

At the time, the Clerk to the Company was Colonel Michael Hardy, who had played international rugby. At one livery function, Michael found himself sitting next to a particularly boring guest who went on at some length about his school and club rugby. Michael listened politely. At last the guest asked Michael, 'Did you play rugger?' Michael replied that he had. 'Oh, who did you play for?' 'England.'

I began to become involved in the Plumbers Company beyond merely supporting the various social functions and became a member of the Technical Committee. It became clear that the Plumbers Company had retained close links with the craft. The members of the livery could be divided into three main groups. There were those who had a craft connection with plumbing in gas or water; those professionally involved with gas or water supply or through architecture or construction and those with family or city links with the company. The Plumbers had long-standing links with the City and Guilds Institute and was building its relationship with the City University and the Technical Committee proposed to the Court that the Company should institute an Annual Lecture.

The Lectures are now an important part of the City calendar and a series of top-flight lecturers have covered a wide range of subjects, some fairly loosely related to plumbing, ranging from regulation of drinking water quality to global sustainability.

As part of its educational commitment, the Company presents a number of awards including the Lilli Sara Barber Memorial Gold Medal to the best young plumber in the country. It also presents three awards to colleges, the Wilkinson Merit Shield, the Award for Excellence in Sheet Leadwork Teaching and the Award for Excellence in Copper Pipework Teaching. Awards are also made to the best engineering apprentices in the Royal Engineers, the Royal Navy and, at my instigation, the Royal Air Force.

The award to the best Army engineering apprentice at Chatham was long-standing and when Admiral Sir John Lea became Master of the Plumbers Company, he persuaded the Court of the Company that it was time to offer a similar award to the best engineering artificer from the training establishment, HMS *Sultan*, on Hayling Island. So when I became Master of the Plumbers in 1995, I put it to the Court that it was high time that we recognised the Royal Air Force in the same way as the Army and the Navy. My RAF rank as a retired Leading Aircraftsmen was some way below that of Sir John Lea but the Court nevertheless agreed. Alan Wollaston and I visited RAF Cosford, near Wolverhampton. We were well received and the prize to the best RAF apprentice is now well-established.

The Plumbers Company also set up the Museum of Plumbing in 1980 in Court Barn at the Singleton Museum in Sussex. It has a splendid collection of plumbing tools and an exhibition illustrating

the role of the plumber and explaining something of water supply and
sewage disposal. Members of the Institute of Plumbing and lecturers
and students from local technical colleges give regular demonstrations
of plumbing skills at Singleton. The Plumbers Company also gives
support to the Ironbridge Industrial Museum in Shropshire.

In 1987, I became a member of the Court of the Company,
known as an Assistant and in October 1995, I was installed as Master
of the Worshipful Company of Plumbers. The year that followed was
hectic. I had retired as Managing Director of North Surrey Water in
July 1995 but was still much involved as Chairman and was also
planning with Deborah our move to Northumberland. There were
many highlights for us both. One was the children's party given by
the Lord Mayor of London in Mansion House in January 1996. I was
able to invite all four grandchildren but as only one adult was allowed
to accompany them, Deborah took them while I spent the Saturday
afternoon choosing CDs. Anna, Lauren, Robbie and Phillipa all wore
fancy dress, there were entertainers and lots to eat and they had a
wonderful time, as did Deborah.

There were also many memorable formal events, including the
banquet given by the Lord Mayor for the Masters of the Livery

*Author's wife and grandchildren at Mansion House, London, Lord Mayor's Children's
Party, January 1996, left to right, Anna, Philipa, Deborah, Robbie and Lauren*

Companies and their spouses and many luncheons and dinners given by other livery companies, as well as hosting the functions of my own Company. Two of these stand out in my memory. The first was the Plumbers Annual Banquet at Mansion House in March 1996 and the other was the Court Ladies Night held in the magnificent Vintners Hall.

For the Annual Banquet, I had to find an outstanding speaker to reply to the toast to 'the Guests'. At the time, Lord Walton of Detchant was Chairman of Convocation at the University of Newcastle upon Tyne. I took him to lunch at the Connaught and persuaded him to undertake the task. The Banquet is a full dress event and it was a great privilege to be the host on such a great occasion in such grand surroundings. The Clerk of the Plumbers Company, Lt Col Antony Paterson-Fox and Mrs Eileen Lilley, the Assistant Clerk to the Company (later to receive the MBE for her services to the Plumbers Company), made sure that I was fully aware of my responsibilities. We had meetings with senior officials of the Corporation of the City of London and a rehearsal to check the sound arrangements and all the other details just before the banquet.

Deborah came with my three daughters and when Lord Walton got up to speak, he began by pointing out that he had been a pupil at Pickering Nook Junior School in County Durham where his father had been headmaster. He went on, 'I know that Jack went to the same school and I understand that his daughters, Wyn and Carole also attended that school. I think I can say with confidence that this is the first time in history that four former pupils of Pickering Nook School have been present at the same banquet in Mansion House'.

There was another special feature of that evening that linked it with Deborah's great grandfather, Sir Thomas White, who was Lord Mayor of London in the 1870s. On an earlier visit to Guildhall, Deborah and I had been shown the file on Sir Thomas and discovered the he had presented the Corporation of the City of London with a set of silver candelabra during his mayoralty. I asked whether it might be possible to have the candelabra on the top table at my Banquet and was delighted when that was agreed. So there was a direct link that night with Deborah's famous ancestor. It was a truly memorable occasion.

The Court Ladies Dinner also had a link to Sir Thomas White, because the Vintners Hall in which it was held was the Hall of the

Vintners Company of which Sir Thomas was a Liveryman. It is one of the most beautiful livery halls in London and again, it was a white tie event. Deborah replied to the toast to 'the Ladies' with an excellent speech and I was very proud of her.

When I ended my year as Master in October 1996, Deborah and I followed the example of Sir Thomas White by giving a pair of silver candlesticks to the Plumbers Company and it always gives me pleasure to see them on the table at a Plumbers Dinner.

My other clubs are mostly connected to cricket. Laleham Cricket Club that I joined in 1962 was an important part of my life for over thirty years. I was a player until the early 1990s, Chairman for a time and President for twelve years. The club lost its ground at Ashford Road, Laleham for housing development at the end of the 1969 season and the prospects for survival did not look good. A suitable site for a new ground had been found at Worple Road in Staines but a great deal of work would be required to turn it into a cricket ground.

South West Suburban Water Company had a reasonable cricket ground at Egham but no longer had a team. I suggested to my boss, Fred Green that we ought to be able to come to an arrangement to allow Laleham to use the ground while a new ground was prepared. He agreed in principle and Dick Faulkner, the President of Laleham CC came to the water company office to meet Fred. They got on well together and Laleham was able to play its home fixtures at Egham in the 1970 and 1971 seasons, allowing the new ground and pavilion at Worple Road to be made ready. We moved to the new ground in April 1972 and that coincided with the first season of Laleham CC in league cricket, when the club became a founder member of the Thames Valley League.

It was a strong league, with outstanding teams like Basingstoke, Reading and High Wycombe and I enjoyed the cricket. My last season of first team league cricket was in 1974 and I became captain of the second eleven in 1975. I had four good years as captain and in 1976, had my best year with the bat. I scored well over a thousand runs, including a couple of centuries. One of those was the highest score of my career when I made 151 not out at Three Bridges in Sussex.

In the early seventies, I also became a member of the MCC, an honour I could scarcely have dreamed of when I began playing senior cricket at Tantobie Cricket Club in 1947. It's easy to mock the old school ties and the old-fashioned world of some members of MCC but the club has been at the heart of cricket almost since the start of organised cricket and I'm very proud of my membership. Perhaps my grandson Robbie Baruch, a keen cricketer at his school in Warwick, will some day join me as a member.

At about the same time as I joined MCC, I also became a member of the Forty Club. This club was founded just before the Second World War to take cricket to the schools. Members have usually played cricket to good club standard and some have played first-class cricket. All are over the age of forty. Some of my friends were closely involved with the club and for a few years, I played a few games a year for teams managed by Duncan Ritchie and Dennis Cornwell, both of whom played for Ashford CC, arch rivals of Laleham. Since moving to Northumberland, Duncan and his wife Joan and Dennis and his wife Rita have some to stay with us on several occasions.

Durham County Cricket Club was another club of which I became a member in the years after I began to play less regularly. After long negotiations, it was agreed that Durham would join the ranks of the first-class counties for the 1992 season. In February 1992, a few weeks before Durham's first season as a first-class county, the club arranged a tour of Zimbabwe and Deborah and I joined a group of twenty or so members on the tour. We saw several games at various grounds in Harare, including at the Harare Sports Club, and went to the eastern highlands near the border with Mozambique for a game at Mutare. Zimbabwe is a truly beautiful country and one can only hope that sanity will return there some day.

One of the bonuses of the tour was that we became friendly with the Chairman of Durham CCC, Don Robson and his wife Jenny. As Leader of Durham County Council and wearing a range of other political hats for many years, Don and Jenny have made enormous contributions to the development of the north-east. But perhaps the achievement of bringing first-class cricket (followed amazingly quickly by test and international cricket), to the region will be Don's most lasting legacy to the part of the country that he loves so much. It has changed the perceptions of the north-east of so many people in the south and given a new sense of identity to a huge number of people. When Durham CCC hosted two matches in the 2000 Cricket World Cup television audiences all over the world had the chance to see the magnificent Riverside ground at Chester-le-Street.

Then on Thursday 5 June 2003, when the second Test Match between England and Zimbabwe began at the Riverside, the dream of Don Robson and of so many people in the region was complete.

When I became a member of Durham in the Minor Counties days, Deborah and I often went to see matches when Durham played at places in the south of England such as Norwich against Norfolk, or at Mildenhall against Suffolk, or St Albans versus Hertfordshire. So when we heard that Durham was seeking acceptance as a first-class county, we were keen to support. Soon after the announcement was made that Durham would become the first new first-class county since Glamorgan just after the First World War, Deborah and I wrote to all those members in the south of England that we could identify, inviting them to a meeting to discuss setting up an organisation of 'Durham exiles'. The response was good and the Dunelm Cricket Society was born. I was elected Chairman with Deborah as Secretary.

The members of the Society had their first dinner at the East India Club in London in 1992 during Durham's first appearance against Middlesex at Lords. Most of the Durham players and directors came and it was a great evening. Don and Jenny Robson were tremendously supportive of the Society from the beginning, and were both at that first dinner. From that night, the dinner has become an annual event, always attended by the players and representatives of the cricket club. The Dunelm Cricket Society continues to work to support the county club and has receptions at various grounds in the south where Durham CCC plays, and generally one at the Chester-le-Street ground of Durham CCC during a home match each season.

Soon after our move to Northumberland in 1996, Deborah and I resigned from office in the Society at a Committee meeting at our home and we were delighted to be presented with an inscribed decanter from the Society. Mike and Mandy Coombs took over as Chairman and Secretary and at the following AGM, I was elected President and Deborah was elected Vice President. It was a real and rare joint honour.

CHAPTER 12

Professional bodies

All professions are conspiracies against the laity
George Bernard Shaw, *The Doctor's Dilemma*, 1913

THE FIRST BODY THAT I joined that was linked professionally to my work was the Coke Oven Managers Association, known as COMA. I became a member soon after beginning to work for the National Coal Board at Norwood Coke Works at Dunston in Gateshead, and the Association was of considerable importance for engineers and scientists working in the coal carbonisation industry at that time. Membership gave me an inkling of the scale of national and international steel-making and the related business of coal carbonisation, especially in India and China.

The Northern Section of the Association held regular meetings at the Three Tuns Hotel in Durham where technical papers were presented and discussed and as I've already mentioned, I gave my first ever paper there in 1958. The prospect of speaking in public for the first time and in front of an audience containing many senior figures in the National Coal Board was somewhat worrying. A friend who was attending the meeting drove me from home in Chester-le-Street to Durham and bought me a vodka and tonic as soon as we arrived. It probably wasn't the most sensible thing to do and over forty years later, would certainly not receive general approval, but those were different times. In the event, everyone was kind and I enjoyed receiving praise afterwards from many people that I'd never spoken to before.

A little later, I had an even more stressful morning in London when I presented a similar paper on my research on phenol removal to a major meeting in Church House, Westminster. I've rarely been more nervous than I was sitting in the front row waiting for the Chairman to finish introducing me, but once I had my first slide on the screen and the lights had been dimmed, I began to enjoy the experience. It seems to me that there is something of the actor in most of us.

On entering the water industry, I joined the Society for Water Treatment and Examination, SWTE. For generations, civil engineers had dominated the UK water industry. They had their own professional body, the Institution of Water Engineers, and although scientists were able to be involved, usually they were seen and felt to be second-class citizens. So the scientists had formed their own society in the fifties with some famous men (the members were almost all men) among its leaders. They included many people I've already mentioned, people like Len Bays from Bristol Water Company, Dr Windle Taylor from the Metropolitan Water Board (MWB), Tom Waterton from Sunderland and South Shields Water Company, Tom Palin from Newcastle and Gateshead Water Company and many others. Everyone made me welcome as a new boy in the industry and Windle, Len and the two Toms eventually became personal friends.

I began to be invited to present papers on the work I was doing on trying to improve water treatment at South West Suburban Water Company. One of these was presented jointly in about 1970 with Professor Ken Ives of University College London and Dr Derek Miller of the then Water Research Association to the Institution of Water Engineers at a meeting at the Institution of Civil Engineers in London. It was a considerable honour when the paper was awarded an Institution prize and we received our awards at a subsequent meeting in Brighton.

The discussion on an earlier paper I presented, this time to the SWTE, taught me an important lesson. I had described in some detail the improvements in water treatment that I had initiated at South West Suburban and afterwards, Tom Palin asked, 'Could the author explain how it was that people living in his company's area received an adequate supply of safe drinking water before he joined the company?' There is a great temptation when we are young to forget the achievements of those who went before us and I was lucky to have a friend able to make me aware of that particular pitfall fairly early in my career.

That reminds me of a story that Leonard Millis told against himself. As a clever young man with a degree in economics and reading for the Bar, he joined the staff of the then Metropolitan Water Board. After a year or two, Leonard felt that his ability was not being properly rewarded and he sought a meeting with the Clerk of the

MWB. Leonard explained how fortunate the MWB was to have available to it the considerable talents of Leonard Millis and that if the MWB was not able to provide him with a position and a salary that was appropriate to those talents, he would have to consider taking those talents elsewhere.

According to Leonard, the Clerk, Francis Stringer, replied, 'Well Mr Millis, you are clearly a young man of exceptional ability and I have no doubt that if you were to leave us, the effectiveness of the Metropolitan Water Board would be somewhat reduced. On the other hand, I must tell you that six million Londoners had been receiving a satisfactory water supply for many years before you joined us and I'm sure that if you were to leave us, those six million Londoners would continue, one way or another, to receive a water supply. Maybe it would be done slightly less well, but I don't think many would notice the difference.'

Dr Windle Taylor, Tom Palin, Tom Waterton, Len Bays and I were all members of the Water Quality Committee of the British Waterworks Association that was chaired by Windle and the meetings could be very funny at times, no quarter being asked or given during our debates. Windle retired from the Metropolitan Water Board at the time of the creation of the Regional Water Authorities in 1974 but I continued to meet him professionally through our membership of the International and British Standards water quality committees as I've already described.

One day in the mid-eighties, Windle said to me, 'I shall be retiring soon from the Council of the Royal Institute of Public Health and Hygiene and I think that they need someone there who knows something about drinking water quality issues. Would you be interested?' 'Yes, of course I would, but don't Council members have to be medically qualified?' 'Most are, but it isn't essential. Let me arrange for you to meet the Chairman.'

So a little later, I was taken to lunch by Dr Hastings Carson, the RIPHH Chairman, with Windle and the Secretary of the Royal Institute, Admiral Bill Waddell. Hastings was an excellent host who evidently had vast experience in public health in the West Indies as well as in the UK. He also turned out to have a keen interest in cricket and was and is a fellow member of MCC. We got on well together and soon afterwards, I was elected a Fellow and co-opted to the Council of the Royal Institute.

I became a member of the Finance and General Purposes Committee of the RIPHH and in 1993 was elected the first non-medical Deputy Chairman of Council, continuing in that role for nine years. In its way, that meeting in 1993 was a dramatic occasion because Dr Enid Vincent was elected to be the first woman Chairman of the Royal Institute. I like to think that Enid and I were an effective team and when she decided to retire from the post, I continued to support her successor, Dr Anthony Golding.

Tony saw the Royal Institute of Public Health and Hygiene through an at times slightly difficult merger with the Society for Public Health, as a result of which the Royal Institute dropped the word 'Hygiene' from the title, becoming the Royal Institute of Public Health, or the RIPH. When Tony retired from the chair in 1999, Dr Michael O'Brien succeeded him. Michael and I were near neighbours in Northumberland and got to know each other well travelling to and from meetings in London.

During Michael's term of office as Chairman of the Royal Institute, Council made the momentous decision to refurbish its premises at 28 Portland Place in London, a Grade 2 listed building that had been originally designed by Robert Adam. The RIPH Council recognised that as little had been spent on the building for years, it was possible that the structure would turn out to be worse than was expected, and there were clear financial risks. On the other hand, repairs would have to be carried out at some time and at the time of the decision the RIPH had no debt and a reasonable investment portfolio. The refurbishment has proved to be a great success at one level, re-creating the beauty of the original building in a way that has impressed everyone who has seen it. Although the cost of the work turned out to be well in excess of the original estimate, in the event, the timing of the sale of equities from the RIPH portfolio was almost perfect. The fall of the stock market in 2001/2002 meant that the value of the portfolio would have fallen dramatically had the RIPH not sold the shares and applied the proceeds to the creation of added value at 28 Portland Place. However, the scale of the excess costs caused the Royal Institute severe cash flow problems.

The RIPH holds 28 Portland Place at a permanent low rent on a 999-year lease signed in 1920, so the premises are practically freehold. On the other hand, the lease provides for the building to be used for residential use and the current use for office purposes is allowed by a licence granted in 1925 but terminable on six months' notice.

This has recently caused problems during the due diligence associated with merger negotiations. Lawyers for the prospective partners suggested that if the landlord were to terminate the licence, ending the ability of the Royal Institute to use the building as offices, 28 Portland Place could have no value. Their logic was that termination of the licence would mean that the lease would revert to the original residential use but they noted that Westminster Council now designates the whole area for institutional office use and would not allow residential use. The merger discussions collapsed, at least ostensibly, on this point but as I write, negotiations with the freeholder seem likely to resolve the dilemma.

In 2002, Michael O'Brien retired as Chairman of the Royal Institute and I was asked if I would be prepared to let my name go forward for possible election to the chair. At first, I said that I thought that I was now too old, but Michael, Dr Hastings Carson and Dr Jim Dunlop persuaded me otherwise and at the Council meeting following the AGM in July 2002, I was elected to be the first non-medical Chairman of the Council of the Royal Institute. It was a great honour, although at the time, I had little idea of the scale of the problems I was to face as Chairman. As a trustee not medically qualified, my election I think signalled the major change in attitudes that has taken place among members of the medical profession and elsewhere in recognising the multi-disciplinary approach needed in finding solutions to problems of public health.

The period since the summer of 2003 has been difficult. For a time, I virtually combined the role of Chief Executive with that of Chairman of Council. This placed an unusual workload on me and on the Chairman of the Executive Committee, John Stevens. During that period, John's background in the City of London and as Chairman of a health authority has been invaluable in our rounds of discussions with the bank manager. We were able to convince him that we could see a workable way forward and as a result, our bank has been supportive. As I write this in late 2005, there are clear signs that a practical solution will be found.

I am proud of having become Chairman of the Royal Institute and of the important role that water and sanitation has played in the improvements in public health in the UK in the past hundred and fifty years or so. But so much needs to be done in the developing world and I am pleased that the Royal Institute is becoming more involved in the world of public health outside the UK.

Throughout my career, I was fortunate to work with and be helped by a number of senior figures. Sir Leonard Millis was one and it was through his links that I became involved in the British Public Works Congress Council. For many years, the Congress ran a major conference and exhibition, first at Olympia in London and later at the National Exhibition Centre near Birmingham. The exhibition attracted exhibitors from manufacturers of all kinds of construction and other equipment and was attended by engineers and other professionals from local government and the utilities. The money generated by the exhibition was used to fund conferences and bursaries for use by the charitable part of the organisation.

In the eighties, I was elected Chairman of the Public Works Congress Council at a time when the organisation was trying to define a new role for itself. Following reorganisations of local government and the utilities that had resulted in dramatic reductions in the numbers of individual municipalities, water undertakings etc, the numbers of delegates to the Public Works Exhibition and Conference had begun to decline. We struggled on until the mid-nineties and attempted to develop a more international role by working with French public works professionals and with the International Public Works Association based in Washington in the United States.

I gave the keynote address (on the subject of privatisation of public services) to a conference in August 1992 in Boston in the US at the invitation of the International Public Works Association. Two months later, in October 1992, the Public Works Congress and Exhibition was held at the National Agricultural Centre at Stoneleigh in Warwickshire. In some ways it was a success.

We succeeded in persuading the Princess Royal to open the Exhibition and she impressed everyone there very much indeed. She was exceptionally generous with her time, visiting every one of the exhibition stands and talking to the exhibitors. We also attracted some excellent speakers to the Congress but it was clear from the numbers attending that the time had come to acknowledge that the role of the Public Works Congress and Exhibition had disappeared at least for the time being.

Also in 1992, I was introduced to Sir Austin Bide who turned out to have a considerable influence on me. Austin had been Chairman

British Public Works Exhibition, with HRH The Princess Royal, Stoneleigh, 1992

of Glaxo, the great pharmaceutical company and by 1992 had become Chairman of Onyx, a waste management company owned, like North Surrey Water, by Compagnie Générale des Eaux. At a meeting of chairmen of companies in the UK within the French group, I met Austin for the first time. In a fairly brief conversation, we discovered a shared concern about the future of the world in the light of the pressures on natural resources and the environment and the massive social and economic inequalities between people in the industrialised countries and those in the rest of the world.

I said, 'What about having lunch together so that we can have a longer chat?' 'Good idea. Where do you suggest?' 'Well, I like the Connaught very much. What about meeting there?' 'My favourite place. It used to be my canteen when I was Chairman of Glaxo.'

So a couple of weeks later, we had lunch at the Connaught Hotel in London. We explored the paradox of the need to reduce pressures on the environment while simultaneously improving the living standards of so many people in the world. We also talked about the hypocrisy of many in the developed world who lecture people in countries such as Brazil about the harm they do by cutting down rain forests when our own prosperity is based to such a large extent on our exploitation of the world's natural resources since at least the start of the eighteenth century.

Towards the end of lunch, Austin said to me, 'Well, Jack, that's been a really interesting chat. You probably don't know it, but Sir Maurice Laing and I have just recently set up a Trust to explore some of these issues in more detail. We've decided to call it the World Humanity Action Trust, to be known as 'WHAT', and I've been made Chairman with Maurice as Vice-Chairman. We've some interesting Trustees on board. People like John Ashworth (then head of the London School of Economics), Peter Jay (the former diplomat and BBC economist), Sir Ghyllian Prance (the head of Kew), Sir Kenneth Newman (former Commissioner of the Metropolitan Police) and Sir John Maddox (the former editor of *Nature*), with Lord Judd (former Head of Oxfam) as our adviser. I wonder if you'd like to join us?'

I said that I'd be delighted and so began a fascinating period of my life in which I had to develop my ideas on a range of things well outside my professional and managerial expertise and experience and be prepared to debate those ideas with some of the sharpest minds around.

It soon became clear to me that the main difficulty lay in the fact that so many people looked only at one element of the overall problem. So-called 'environmentalists' were much more clear about the things they wanted to stop happening than they were about what they positively thought should be done. On the other hand, many politicians and economists seemed ready to leave the future to the markets, ignoring the fact that the operation of market forces within the existing systems of valuation of natural resources was largely responsible for the unsustainable state that the world had reached. What Peter Jay and John Ashworth were fond of referring to as 'first order approaches to problem solving'.

For some time, WHAT generated more heat than light. One of our difficulties was that each Trustee had a slightly different idea of what we were trying to do. We decided that we needed a Director to give a stronger focus to our work and we recruited Dr Eileen

Buttle to that new post. Eileen and I had known each other fairly well a few years earlier when she was at the Natural Environment Research Council (NERC) at a time when I was trying to extract funding from NERC for the Freshwater Biological Association. She had done a good job there in often difficult circumstances.

In an attempt to make progress, we agreed to invite James Morgan, a BBC journalist, to consider writing a personal view of the issues we were debating. He joined us at a weekend meeting at the Police College near Basingstoke in Hampshire. He listened to our discussions, and then had a series of one-to-one meetings with Trustees, after which he wrote a book called *The Last Generation*, published in 1999.

At about this time, Eileen Buttle decided that running WHAT was not for her and she left. I was sad to see her go because I had great respect for her ability, but we were fortunate to recruit Dr Peter Warren as her replacement. Peter had just recently retired as Secretary of the Royal Society and he brought to our discussions a great understanding of both science and decision-making processes.

When Sir Austin stepped down as Chairman of WHAT, John Ashworth replaced him and we soon agreed that we should try a different approach. We identified three important environmental problem areas and decided to appoint three commissions to consider the changes required to the way in which such areas are managed, in order to improve the chances of the world having a sustainable future. The subjects chosen were agricultural genetic diversity, marine fish stocks and water. All three are natural resources, examples of what are often described as global commons. We hoped that the reports of the three commissions would contain some common factors pointing towards the changes required to the overall governance systems through which mankind manages itself.

I became lead Trustee on the water commission and we assembled a strong and varied international group under the chairmanship of John Rodda, a well-known water engineer. In addition to water engineers and scientists, the commission also contained several others from outside the narrow technical field, including an American academic lawyer and a French journalist.

The first meeting was held in Oxford over two days and the first task at that meeting was to change the assumptions of the water specialist commission members. They arrived thinking that they would be giving their professional views on the solutions to the water

problems of the world. I began by suggesting that many groups had
produced reports on those lines over several decades. It seemed fair
to think that the water specialists present would agree broadly on the
things that should be done, as there had been general agreement
among professionals for decades.

The question WHAT was asking was different. We wanted to
know why those things that seemed obvious to the experts were not
being done. We wanted the commission to advise on whether their
consensus stood up to examination from a broader perspective,
including social, environmental, economic and political issues. We
wanted the commission to think about water in an integrated way
and to identify not only what should be done, but also the steps
needed to make these things happen, leading to a sustainable future.
I described this as the governance dimension to the problem.

By late 1999, all three commissions were nearing completion of
their tasks and WHAT invited Ian Christie and Michael Carley to
work together on producing a paper identifying common governance
principles from the individual reports of the three commissions.
However, health problems led to Peter Warren stepping down as
Director and at a meeting of Trustees in December 1999, John
Ashworth announced that other commitments meant that he would
have to stand down as Chair of WHAT from April 2000.

He proposed that I become Chair Designate with a view to taking
the Chair in April 2000. In March 2000, the Trustees endorsed this
and a hectic period of preparation of the completed work for
publication followed. Sir John Maddox, with his journalistic experience, was a key figure in this phase and his son did a splendid job of
editing the papers.

There was a United Nations meeting on sustainability scheduled
for September 2000 in New York and it was decided to launch the
WHAT report in New York to coincide with that meeting. The
time-scale was short but it was good to have a deadline. Without it,
I doubt whether we should ever have agreed the details of the text
and the launch arrangements, especially as the new Director of
WHAT resigned soon after I took over the chair. That left us with
one full-time member of staff, Aretha Moore, and a part-time
Treasurer, Nigel Parfitt. But in the summer of 2000, Peter Warren
agreed to become a Trustee as did Lord Judd, who had been a
consultant to WHAT at an earlier stage. With his experience as a

former head of OXFAM and his political background as a minister in the seventies, he was an invaluable asset.

Everyone worked very hard to ensure that all the hard work of the previous two or three years wasn't wasted and the support of the two founders of WHAT, Sir Austin Bide and Sir Maurice Laing was constant and immensely important to me. Incidentally, Sir Austin was also, I believe, largely responsible for me being invited to become a Companion of the Institute of Management, now the Chartered Management Institute, a great honour that I much appreciated.

Aretha Moore performed administrative miracles and the WHAT report, called 'Governance for a Sustainable Future' and containing the reports of the three commissions as well as the integrative report by Ian Christie and Michael Carley, was launched in September 2000 live in New York with a simultaneous satellite link to audiences in London and Brussels. It went well and we felt that we had iterated a set of documents that might make a difference by opening up a new set of possibilities that would be debated in various fora around the world.

One consequence of the launch was an approach from UNED UK (United Nations Environment and Development), a part of United Nations Association Great Britain and Ireland, UNA. I was asked whether the arguments in the WHAT report could be used by UNED in the preparation of briefing material for the UN and the UK Government in the run-up to the Earth Summit on Sustainable Development to be held in 2002 in Johannesburg.

Of course, that was exactly what we had hoped would happen and Peter Warren and I began to work with Derek Osborn, the chair of UNED and the Director, Felix Dodds. Peter Warren and I joined the UNED Executive Committee (later called Stakeholder Forum for our Common Future) and a short time afterwards, WHAT merged with UNA. It was the formal end of an important part of my life, although I was able to play a small part at the Earth Summit in Johannesburg as part of the Stakeholder Forum delegation and I continued to be involved with the cause of sustainability as a member of the Executive Committee of Stakeholder Forum until the end of 2004.

Among other professional involvements, I was President of the Institution of Water Officers in 1992 and later was made an Honorary Member. There was also my period as President of the Freshwater Biological Association described in another chapter.

CHAPTER 13

University links and the Return of the Native (apologies to Thomas Hardy)

... The long, laborious road, dry, empty and white

Thomas Hardy, *The Return of the Native*

ONE OF THE CONSEQUENCES of my work for WHAT and Stakeholder Forum was a stronger link with the University of Newcastle through contacts with people in the University working on governance-linked issues. Individuals like Ella Ritchie, Enda O'Connell, Tony O'Donnell and Julie Trottier were interested in the work we had done in WHAT and shared many of the views on integrated or 'joined-up' thinking in relation to sustainability that had crystallised in my mind.

For many years, I had attended the annual meetings and dinners in Newcastle of Convocation, the statutory body to which all graduates of the University and of King's College, Newcastle, belong. Maybe this was because a part of me would have liked to experience the academic life. In a way, the Freshwater Biological Association had filled a similar function in enabling me to enjoy some vicarious pleasure in my relationships with genuine researchers.

In the early 1990s, Newcastle University began to recognise that it had a considerable asset in the shape of the approximately 100,000 graduates of the University out there in the community, an argument that a few of us had been making for some time. An Alumni Association was formed under the chairmanship of Nick Richardson, a biologist and Union Society President in the 1970s. I became part of the Alumni Development Group, and Chris Cox was recruited by the University to a full-time role as head of a new Alumni Office. We began to think about ways of building relationships with alumni in terms of providing better services to them and of devising ways in which they could help the University. By 1999, Chris Cox and his team, with support from the members of the Alumni Development Group, had begun a direct appeal to alumni for financial support for the University. This appeal is growing year on year and is helping

166

the University, for example, by providing bursaries and a 'hardship fund'.

In the nineties, the annual meeting and dinner of Convocation was extended into an alumni weekend that varied in content from year to year. We had visits to the opera at the Theatre Royal in Newcastle, river trips from Newcastle to the mouth of the Tyne and back. There were also reunions of year and subject groups and the annual Convocation Lecture became firmly established in the University calendar. The construction of a database of alumni began and this became a valuable source of information for the alumni fund appeal. It also enabled the creation of a group of people prepared to act as specialist mentors to students interested in their field, supporting the work of the Careers Service.

I had been appointed Chair of the Careers Advisory Board in the mid nineties, a group led by the Director of the Careers Service, and composed of a mixture of academics and people from various commercial and industrial backgrounds both regionally and nation-ally. The Careers Service at Newcastle has become recognised as one of the very best in the country under first, Dr Richard Firth and later, Cathryn Harvey, both completely dedicated to the provision of a first-class service to students. Increasingly, this involved Cathryn in devising some imaginative partnership schemes with companies such as BT to find additional funding for the service.

My involvement with the University increased in 1998 when the Vice-Chancellor, James Wright asked me to become a trustee of the University Development Trust and I attended my first meeting on 1 November 1998 at Close House. The mansion of Close House was then owned by the University but has subsequently been sold. The Trust manages considerable assets given to the University by a number of benefactors, two of the largest being the Robinson Library Fund and bequests from the popular Tyneside novelist, Catherine Cookson.

Sometime in the second half of 1998, I was having lunch with some Royal Institute of Public Health colleagues at the Royal Society of Medicine in London when Lord Walton came over to our table and said, 'Hello' to the group. He then said to me, 'Could we have a quick word?' We had known each other quite well for some years and he had replied on behalf of the guests at the Plumbers Banquet at Mansion House in 1996 when I was Master but it was a total surprise to me when he said, 'I'll soon have done ten years as Chairman of Convocation at Newcastle and I wonder whether you might be interested in taking over when I retire next year?' I was enormously flattered as every Chairman of Convocation that I could think of had been a distinguished academic and I certainly do not come into that category. Somehow, I managed to reply that I'd be delighted and honoured to accept the post if the members of Convocation were to elect me. John Walton said, 'Well, I obviously can't promise anything but I do have a few contacts and if you are interested, I'll let it be known.'

For several months, I heard nothing and almost forgot about the meeting. Indeed on the rare occasions that it came into my mind, I began to wonder whether I'd simply misunderstood the conversation with John Walton. Then, in late spring 1999, I had a call from Derek Nicholson, the then Registrar of Newcastle University. He told me that Lord Walton would complete ten years as Chairman of Convocation in the summer. Derek went on, 'Are you interested in having your name put forward as a candidate for election?' I replied, 'If you think that as a non-academic I'll be acceptable to Convocation, yes. It would be a great honour.'

At the meeting of Convocation on 5 June 1999, Lord Walton stood down as Chairman. Dr Lorna Rozner, a friend from the early days of the Graduate Society, proposed my name and as it turned out that I was the only candidate nominated, I was elected Chairman of Convocation.

One of the pleasant duties of the Chairman of Convocation is to introduce the speaker at the annual Convocation Lecture that always follows the meeting of Convocation. In June 2000, I had the honour of chairing the lecture given by Chris Patten, fairly recently elected Chancellor of the University to succeed Viscount Ridley. There was a slight coincidence in those links in that I had had contact with Nicholas Ridley, the younger brother of Viscount Ridley, when he was Secretary of State for the Environment during the passage of the water privatisation bill, and once or twice, with Chris Patten when he followed Nicholas Ridley at DoE in that same period. The lecture by Chris Patten gave us a fascinating glimpse of the way in which the European Union works. He dealt calmly and expertly with the one or two aggressive questioners and greatly impressed the vast majority of the audience.

We always try to find a lecturer who will bring something different to the occasion and we succeeded brilliantly in 2001 when Matt Ridley, son of Lord Ridley, and a distinguished scientist and journalist in his own right, lectured on recent developments in genetics. He spoke with great authority and demonstrated his considerable ability to communicate a complex subject in a way that was intelligible to a largely lay audience. Matt Ridley was followed as the Convocation Lecturer in 2002 by John Bridge, the Head of One NorthEast, who described the work of his agency in designing a policy to help the regeneration of the region. The choice of John was influenced by the involvement of the University and One North East in the joint bid by Newcastle and Gateshead to become European Capital of Culture in 2003. Sadly for the north-east region, it was announced in June 2003 that Liverpool had been selected for the title.

James Wright had retired in 2000 and been replaced by Christopher Edwards as Vice-Chancellor. Professor John Goddard, who became Deputy Vice-Chancellor, had worked hard for a long time to build relationships with regional businesses and local government and Christopher Edwards encouraged these links and quickly became involved personally. The University was playing a full part in the preparation of the Capital of Culture bid, so it was fitting that John Bridge should explain the role of his agency to a university audience. His lecture, I think, opened many eyes to the wider regional environment in which the University operates.

The Capital of Culture bid was also a factor in the choice of Sir Thomas Allen as Lecturer for 2003. When I first met Deborah in 1972, I remember her mentioning a young baritone called Tom Allen, already becoming famous, and later to become Sir Thomas Allen. Tom had left his home in County Durham to study music in London and as a student, had for a time had a room in the home in Barnes where Deborah lived with her mother. She was clearly impressed by Tom but it was many years before we all met. Eventually, Deborah and I met Tom at Covent Garden when we went to hear him in *Cosi fan Tutte*. Then after moving to Northumberland, we met regularly at musical events organised by the Samling Foundation, a charity of which Tom is Patron, based in Hexham and devoted to developing young talent in the arts, chiefly music.

I wrote to Tom asking him if he would be prepared to give the 2003 Convocation Lecture and to my delight, he agreed. His lecture was tremendously popular and told us something of the stresses that can arise between operatic directors, conductors and singers. It was a brilliant performance. At the Convocation Dinner that followed, we had arranged for some musical entertainment to be provided by Johnny Handle of the famous north-east folk group, the High Level Ranters with David Newey and Christi Andropolis from the newly-established folk music course at the University. They were only supposed to do three songs but on the spur of the moment, I asked Johnny Handle to sing that wonderful local song, 'Geordie's Lost his Penker'. He agreed and it was great fun to join in the chorus with Tom Allen and Christopher Edwards. Afterwards Tom and his wife, Jeannie, stayed with Deborah and me at Hedley to round off a wonderful weekend.

For 2004 we invited Baroness Warnock, the great moral philosopher, to present the Convocation Lecture. She chose as a title 'The Good and the Natural' and her lecture was all that we'd hoped for – thoughtful, stimulating and at times, provocative. It was a privilege to meet her.

Then, for 2005, Lord Judd agreed to give the Convocation Lecture, choosing as his title. 'Security and the Battle for Hearts and Minds'. Frank had become a good friend when we had worked together in the World Humanity Action Trust and his subject could not have been more topical, given the continuing debate about the Iraq war, and legislation being introduced by the UK Government. Once again, there was a large audience for the Lecture and an excellent presentation was followed by a first-class debate. Somewhat to my relief as Chairman, although the debate covered a wide range of issues on which many people felt passionately, it was always conducted in a reasonable way, in large part due to the obvious sincerity and political skill of the speaker.

My latest link with the University has been through an invitation to join the new Development Council, chaired by Sir Terence Harrison, with the task of raising money for the University from philanthropic sources. The main early focus is on supporting the Partners Programme in the University that had been introduced largely through the drive of Pro-Vice-Chancellor Madeleine Atkins (who has since left Newcastle to become Vice-Chancellor of

Professor Christopher Edwards, Lord Judd and the author at the 2005
Newcastle Convocation Lecture

Coventry University). The Partners Programme aims to give opportunities to attend Newcastle University to young people from economically deprived areas of the region who would not normally think of themselves as potential Newcastle graduates. Candidates for the programme are put through a special induction process, and this will have to be expanded to meet the growing target being set. Some might think that this is an example of what is often described as 'dumbing down' of education. The evidence that has come from the groups of students who graduated in 2003, 2004 and 2005 via the scheme indicates that their results and drop-out rate compare favourably with those obtained by students recruited by more conventional methods. So there are big opportunities for the University to help itself and in so doing, play a further part in the regeneration of the region.

At a meeting of the Court of the University in the autumn of 2004, it was agreed that the University would establish a new award to recognise contributions to the University by non-academics. It was decided that the award would be described as an Honorary Fellowship of the University and at the meeting on 6 May 2005, the Court agreed on the first six recipients of the new honour and I was delighted to be among those six names. Then, at a ceremony at the University on 10 October 2005, I was introduced in flattering terms by Professor Paul Younger. I was then presented with my Honorary Fellowship parchment by the Chancellor of the University, Lord Patten. It was an important occasion for me and for Deborah that we both enjoyed very much.

In the early 1990s, as I approached retirement, Deborah and I began to think more about the possibility of moving from Surrey. I'd always had a fairly vague feeling that I would quite like to return to my north-east roots in retirement and Deborah had grown more and more attached to Northumberland and Durham through our increasingly frequent visits to see my mother living in Tanfield Lea, near Stanley in County Durham.

By that time, my links with the north were growing beyond the University. In addition to being Chairman of Durham County Cricket Club, Don Robson was also Leader of Durham Council and we'd met Don and Jenny Robson on the tour of Zimbabwe by Durham CCC in February 1992. A few months after the tour, I received a phone call from Don. He said, 'The County Council is setting up a company to be owned by the Council to manage waste management in the county. The company has to operate at arms' length from the Council, so we need a Board of independent directors. We'd like to have you as a director because of your environmental background and your roots in the area. Are you interested?' 'I'm certainly interested but I'm going to be working for North Surrey at Staines for another three years and I'd have to get permission from Compagnie Générale des Eaux who own North Surrey. And there would be a potential conflict of interest because Générale des Eaux has a subsidiary, Onyx, operating in waste management.' 'I know all that, but the real conflicts of interest only arise when links like that aren't known so I don't see that need be a problem.'

That had long been my own view so I went to my French boss, Jean Claude Banon, explained the invitation I'd received and he promptly agreed that I could accept. So one morning a short time afterwards, I caught the 7.30 a.m. train from King's Cross to Durham for my first meeting of the Board of Durham County Waste Management. I met the Chairman, Peter Carr, Dr Ralph Iley, recently retired from the Cookson Group, and Richard Harbottle, an

Newcastle University group at the Honorary Fellowships Ceremony in October 2005. Back row, left to right, Professor Paul Younger, Reay Atkinson, Derek Nicholson, Registrar, John Hogan, the author, David Wilson and Professor John Burn. Front row, left to right, Florence Kirkby, Vice-Chancellor, Professor Christopher Edwards, Chancellor, Lord Patten, Chairman of Council, Olivia Grant and Brian Shefton

Retirement from North Surrey Water, author and Deborah, July 1995

accountant. Peter was a former civil servant much involved in regional economic regeneration while Ralph was an old friend who had been a member of the former Northumbrian Water Authority and had represented the authority on the Council of the Water Research Centre, where we had been colleagues before water privatisation. Tony Ewin, a solicitor working for the County Council was the fifth non-executive director and provided a valuable link with the Council as well as keeping us right on legal requirements. He balanced his duties as a director of the company with his Council responsibilities most effectively.

Waste management has changed considerably in the years since Durham County Waste Management was set up. There has been a huge increase in regulation from both the European Union and the UK Government and strong pressure to move away from use of landfill towards reuse and recycling. The company has also had to solve some unusual financial problems.

All of the original staff of the company transferred from Durham County Council bringing with them their rights to inflation-linked pensions based on final salary. They couldn't remain members of the local government scheme so a new pension scheme had to be set up. As the staff did not bring with them from the County Council any pension fund assets, the new scheme was dramatically under-funded from the start and therefore, has required substantial topping-up.

A further financial complication arose from the fact that although the company had to operate at arms' length from the County Council, under Treasury rules any borrowing by the company was counted against the borrowing limit imposed on the County Council. This was interpreted as meaning that the company couldn't borrow. So we had to find ways of meeting the pension liability we had inherited with no assets transferred from the County Council at the same time as we funded our capital expenditure out of revenue. Somehow, we have managed to balance all of these pressures, not without our share of crises, and the company is still growing and still developing innovative approaches to waste management. It has been fun and through it all, Peter Carr and I have developed a firm friendship.

My involvement with Durham County Waste Management and the University of Newcastle upon Tyne together with our member-ship of Durham County Cricket Club were all factors that made Deborah and me think seriously about moving north after my retirement. We began to look at houses when we visited my mother in Tanfield Lea but for some time, couldn't find anything we both liked.

Then in the summer of 1994, while we were with my mother for a few days, I bought the local evening paper and in the classified section under 'Land for Sale' I saw a three-line advert for a half acre site with planning consent in Hedley on the Hill. I remembered Hedley from my cycling days at school as a pretty village with fantastic views.

I said to Deborah, 'Let's drive over and look at the site. Hedley isn't very far from my mother at Tanfield Lea'. She agreed so I rang the number in the advert and arranged to meet the seller the next day. Hedley is about 800 feet above sea level. It can sometimes be windy and occasionally it is literally in the clouds but we arrived on a wonderful July day. We got out of the car and could see the Cheviot Hills clearly to the north as well as west up the Tyne valley beyond Hexham and over towards the coast in the east. We both fell in love with the place and in less than a minute, we'd decided that this was where we wanted to live in our retirement.

We agreed a price and visited the Tynedale planners at Hexham to look at the existing outline planning consent. There, we were given the name of the architect in Chester-le-Street, John Dawson. Deborah called him from the car and arranged for us to see him an hour later. We liked the basic design but wanted to increase the size of the house. The architect agreed to produce a revised design and Tynedale planners then said that we should have to make a fresh planning application. While this was moving forward, I had a call one Sunday morning from our architect.

John Dawson said, 'I thought you ought to know that the company selling your site at Hedley has just gone into liquidation.' I asked, 'Does this mean that the deal may not go ahead?' 'No. It means that you'll be buying from the liquidator and it's possible that you could buy it for a lower price.'

Deborah and I discussed this and decided that we thought we had agreed a fair price for the land and we didn't want to run any risk of losing it so we confirmed to the liquidator that we were standing by our original offer. The purchase was completed in early January 1995 and the new planning consent was granted in May 1995. We then talked to several builders and signed the contract to build the house in August with Bill Quigley, a builder from Esh Winning, near Durham. I had retired as Managing Director of North Surrey Water Company at the end of July 1995 and we put our house in Curley Hill Road, Lightwater for sale through an estate agent in early August. We then went off on holiday with daughter Jill and her family, husband Andy, children Philippa and Robbie and our friend Gillian Mason, to the Dordogne in France.

In less than a week, we'd sold the house to a couple who wanted to move in quickly. Building work on our new house was not due to start until October so we had a problem. We solved it by renting a furnished house in Chobham in Surrey for six months and putting our furniture into storage. In other circumstances, we might have looked to rent a house near Hedley but I was still at that stage spending a lot of time at North Surrey and was just about to start my year as Master of the Worshipful Company of Plumbers with all of the commitments in London that that implied. So we decided to take a pleasant house in The Avenue, on the outskirts of the village of Chobham and enjoyed a happy few months there.

Eventually, we moved into the house at Hedley on the Hill that we'd decided to call Laleham House as a link with the Surrey cricket club where I'd spent so many happy times. We moved in on Friday 19 April 1996. The builders hadn't finished and I had a series of meetings in London during the whole of the following week. I arrived back at Hedley on the following Saturday evening to find that Deborah had performed miracles in turning the house into a home.

Our time at Hedley has been another happy period in our lives. My mother lived only a few miles away at Tanfield Lea and for a time, she was able to enjoy her frequent visits to Hedley and car trips around the Durham dales that she'd always loved. Sadly, following an accident, my mother became unable to look after herself at home and we had to look for a nursing home able to provide her with twenty-four-hour care. After looking at several, we found her a place in a nursing home converted from my old primary school at Pickering Nook. From the window of her large room, she could see

Deborah with Anna, Carole and Lauren at Hexham races

across the fields to the house at Clough Dene where she, my father and I had lived for many years. That gave my mother much pleasure and there were several poems that she loved to have me read to her. Her favourite was Shelley's 'To a Skylark', perhaps partly because it brought back happy memories of her time at Tanfield School, cut short far too soon because her parents couldn't afford to keep her there beyond the age of fourteen. My mother died in her sleep at Pickering Nook in December 1999 in her ninety-fifth year.

Before Deborah told her mother, Evelyn, that we planned to move north, we were worried about her possible reaction. We needn't have been. To our great pleasure, Evelyn's response was to say, 'I always thought that you would want to do that'. We were then extremely lucky to find Howdon Dene, a country house near Corbridge that had been converted into rooms and apartments. At first, Evelyn had a small cottage in the grounds. That meant that she was able to keep her pet poodle with her but after surgery a few years later, she needed a higher level of support. She moved into a lovely room on the ground floor in the main house and we took over looking after her dog. Her room was large with a wonderful view over the large grounds of the house stretching south to the River Tyne. In the years she spent at Howdon Dene until her death in January 2001, Evelyn was as happy as at any time in the nearly thirty years that I knew her.

For several years after our move to Hedley on the Hill, I was still spending a great deal of time in London. I was still actively involved with water as Chairman of the North Surrey and Tendring Hundred Water companies as well as with the RIPH and WHAT. In addition, for the first few months, I was completing my year as Master of the Plumbers Company, and so was in London for many meetings of my own Livery Company and as a guest at many functions of other companies. As a result, Deborah was often at home alone. Given her London background, life in rural Northumberland might have been difficult had she sat back and waited for something to happen. Deborah isn't one to do that. She wanted to become part of the village, which isn't the easiest thing in the world to do. The balance between being ready to be involved in village activities and being seen as pushy can be tricky to achieve but Deborah did it. We've made many new friends in the area and have never regretted the move.

Hedley on the Hill is small, with a population of less than two hundred people. There are no shops but there is a real village pub, the Feathers Inn. When Deborah and I visited Hedley during the winter of 1995/96 to check on the progress being made in building our house, we usually managed to look in at the Feathers, sometimes having lunch there on a Saturday. In that way, we began slowly to get to know a few people from the village.

Quite soon after we moved into Laleham House, as I was leaving the house one morning, I met the postman and I could see that he was carrying a copy of *Jazz Journal*. I'd subscribed to the magazine for many years and as it has only a small circulation, I assumed it was for me. I said, 'That'll be my *Jazz Journal*, I think'. The postman looked at it and replied, 'No. That's for Mr Tate around the corner'. So to my great surprise, I discovered that there were two of us in the village who subscribed to *Jazz Journal*, very much a minority interest publication. When I got to know John Tate a little later, I found that we were both great admirers of the singing of Lee Wiley, someone few people now remember, but nevertheless, a great singer from the thirties through into the fifties.

Having been brought up on a market garden, I'd long ago decided that gardening was too much like hard work, so leek clubs were not for me but in the autumn of 1996, Deborah joined the Feathers Inn Leek Club. At first, she had the benefit of some help from Peter Jeffery, who lives a few miles away at Burnopfield and is the son of my cousin Ron, both good leek growers. Deborah picked up the essentials quickly and she soon became a great enthusiast. She won prizes for her onions and marrows and in 2001 she won the cup for the best leek in the show. Later that year, she was elected Chairman of the Leek Club, as far as I know, the only woman to be Chairman of a Leek Club, such a traditionally male-dominated part of north-east culture.

My involvement with the Leek Club has been limited to supporting the many functions arranged through the club and the Feathers Inn. These include the monthly domino competitions throughout the winter, race nights, ten-pin bowling and car treasure hunts. A particular highlight of the year is the annual summer barbecue. The village marquee is erected and a bar set up alongside the tables groaning with home-made salads etc. There is a cricket pitch available (with a soft ball!) and croquet competition, but most people are content to sit around in their deck-chairs, eating, drinking and chatting. And the sun almost always shines.

Deborah and I had both joined the Taverners while living in Surrey and soon after moving north, Deborah was asked to become Chairman of the Northumberland and Durham Region of the Lady Taverners while I joined the committee of the Northumberland and Durham Lords Taverners. For a long time, Deborah organised a series of fund-raising events for the Lady Taverners. Those events always had strong support from people in Hedley and were often followed by a party at our house starting at something like half past one or two o'clock in the morning. In recent years, The Taverners has allocated many specially adapted minibuses to schools and other bodies in the north-east working with children and young people with special needs as well as presenting cricket kit to junior cricket teams in deprived areas. Her work for the Taverners has given Deborah great satisfaction and some justifiable pride.

Although we were very happy living in Hedley, Deborah and I both love the sea and we began to think about buying a holiday home near the sea. After some searching we found a former fisherman's cottage for sale in the tiny village of Low Hauxley on the beautiful Northumberland coast a mile or two south of Amble and less than forty miles from Hedley. We bought it in 2001 and Peter Ashworth, an architect friend in Hedley, designed some alterations that enabled us to convert it into a delightful little house. It is in a small square of terraced cottages and the front door is less than fifty yards from the beach. We've made more new friends in Hauxley and look forward to the annual Fun Day at the end of August when the village is crowded with visitors buying bric-à-brac and home-made cakes, trying their strength, breaking crockery and eating burgers and sausages from the barbecue while the children enter the sandcastle competition on the beach. Low Hauxley is a perfect place to relax and is popular with several members of the family.

At about the same time as buying the cottage at Hauxley, we decided that as we visit Barbados every year, it made sense to buy a share of an apartment on the island. We now have an apartment for four weeks each year at the Crane, on the south-east of the island, away from the crowds on the west coast. It can sleep six, has three bathrooms and a pool, and it's a great pleasure to be able to entertain family and friends there. It's an added pleasure when we visit the

Author's wife, Deborah, with Floss raising funds for the Lady Taverners at Northumberland County Show, Corbridge

island that we have good friends living there like Ben Arrindell and his wife Shelley, and Cammie and Phyllis Smith. Ben and I played cricket together for Staines and Laleham when he was training in London and he is now Managing Partner of the Bridgetown office of the accountants, Ernst and Young. We got to know Cammie and Phyllis through another former Laleham cricketer, Mike Wilkinson. Cammie played for West Indies in the early sixties and was for a time President of the Barbados Cricket Association. Through his kindness, Deborah and I have watched several West Indies Test Matches from the comfort of the President's Box at Kensington Oval in Bridgetown. Cammie and Phyllis and Ben and Shelley are more of the many special friends we've made through cricket.

In my youth, I'd been taken to local meetings of the National Secular Society, NSS, in Newcastle by my grandfather and had become a member a little later. For various reasons, mainly carelessness, my subscriptions to the NSS and to the long-established journal, the *Freethinker*, lapsed some time after my move south but soon after my return to my roots, I re-joined the NSS and renewed my subscription to the *Freethinker*. A short time later, I saw a notice in the *Freethinker* about a meeting of North East Humanists, NEH, and joined that local group as well as becoming a member of the British Humanist Association, BHA.

My youthful atheism had consisted of little more than a generalised opposition to religion and I'd tended to think of humanists as having invented the word to avoid having to call themselves atheists. Once having become actively involved, I quickly realised that I had been wrong. The people that I got to know at the monthly meetings of NEH at the Literary and Philosophical Society in Newcastle came from a wide range of backgrounds but most shared the view that humanism was about the rights of all individuals to believe or not to believe while campaigning for a world in which human rights are respected. I have no wish to try to meddle in any way with the beliefs of an individual. At the same time, it is important to be free to criticise the group application of religious dogma when it interferes with the human rights of others. There are many examples of religious dogma adversely affecting human rights. They include the inferior status of women and of homosexuals in all major religions and the continuing discrimination against the Dalits in India resulting from the caste system, in spite of civil laws that, in theory, make such discrimination illegal.

Ideally, there should be separation of church and state preventing religious laws such as Sharia law taking precedence over civil laws. The appalling consequences for individuals that often follow the application of religious laws are still being seen and have been demonstrated recently by women being sentenced to death by stoning for committing adultery, Dr Younus Sheikh sentenced to death in Pakistan for blasphemy (released after a three-year campaign) and rape victims being imprisoned for 'fornication'.

In the middle of the summer of 2001, I was asked if I would accept nomination for the Executive Committee of the BHA. The Chairman of NEH, Professor Colin Gallagher, had been an Executive Committee member and Deputy Chairman of BHA for several years and was stepping down. So he and Barrie and Jean Berkeley, all of whom put in an enormous amount of work in the cause of humanism, persuaded me to put my name forward. Barrie and Jean were not long retired, having lived for a time in New York where Barrie worked for an oil company. They had suffered the tragedy of the loss of their son on his way to spend the Christmas holiday with his parents in the crash of the Pan Am flight from London to New York in 1988 at Lockerbie. After retirement, they bought a delightful house in the Tyne Valley and they provide much of the energy that drives forward the NEH.

Once nominated, I discovered that there were usually more vacancies on the BHA Executive Committee than there were candidates. That proved to be the case and in the autumn of 2001, I was elected to the BHA Executive Committee for a three-year term. There was just one snag. The meetings were generally held on Saturdays in London. In the summer of 1996, I'd bought a season ticket to watch Sunderland, the team that my father had supported and that I had supported from 1937 when they beat Preston North End at Wembley by three goals to one to win the FA Cup. As a result, I got to know another Hedley resident, Mike Turnbull and his sons Matthew and Paul, all Sunderland supporters in a village that is a Newcastle United stronghold. Mike and I have become firm friends and we've renewed our tickets each year subsequently through relegation, the despair of the promotion play-off final at Wembley against Charlton Athletic in 1998, promotion in 1999, relegation again in 2003, promotion again in 2005 and once again, relegation in 2006. In my first year on the BHA Committee, BHA meetings meant that there were some occasions when I had to miss a match. But when we came to agree dates for meetings in my second year, I was able to make sure that there were few clashes of dates.

In November 2001, there was a BHA strategy weekend in Birmingham with the first meeting of the newly elected Executive Committee on Sunday after the strategy meeting. At dinner on the Saturday evening, Chris Butterworth, the Chair of the Committee, asked me if I'd be prepared to stand for election as Vice-Chair. I said that it didn't seem right for me to stand for that position so soon. Chris replied that there were several new members of the Committee and she thought that I was the right person for the job, so in spite of my misgivings, I agreed to stand and was elected.

Since then, the BHA has been changing quite rapidly. A new Chief Executive, Hanne Stinson, had been appointed at about the time of my first meeting. She attended the strategy weekend and took office at the end of 2001. I learned that, for many years, the BHA had functioned to a large extent through volunteers. They were members, but in some ways carried out tasks voluntarily that in a larger organisation would have been the responsibility of paid staff. By 2001, the BHA staff was growing and almost without realising it, the organisation was in transition. That was creating a few tensions because one or two of the long-serving volunteers still saw themselves as having a direct operational role. That sometimes resulted in staff feeling that they had more than one boss, something that is clearly wrong. On the other hand, those volunteers undoubtedly had and still have much to offer the BHA so Hanne and Chris had a slight problem from time to time. Happily, everyone made the necessary adjustments, although as in any organisation in a period of transition, tensions still arose from time to time.

One example lies in the field of what the BHA refers to as 'ceremonies'. These include secular weddings, baby-naming occasions and funerals. All are becoming more commonplace, but humanist funerals have grown particularly rapidly in recent years. At first, it seems to have been organised on a totally ad hoc basis, but by the mid-nineties, a structure was beginning to emerge. In several parts of the country, individuals began to set up loose networks of people prepared to carry out ceremonies and in the case of funerals, to establish links with local undertakers.

Gradually, the BHA recognised a need for standards to be set and training and accreditation of officiants began to be introduced. For a time, much of this seems to have remained somewhat ad hoc and there were differences in different parts of the country but the development of quality assurance schemes and of a disciplinary procedure began to bring things together.

However, this all cost money and like most charities, the BHA was and is always short of that. So a voluntary levy on the fees paid to officiants for their services was introduced. By the time that I joined the Executive Committee, it was becoming clear that the cost of providing and administering training, accreditation and the rest exceeded the income generated to the BHA. Some of us argued that this could not be allowed to continue for much longer because it could be contrary to our duties under charity law. So the BHA introduced a £5 levy on each ceremony. All officiants are self-employed and there is no system of checking the number of ceremonies they carry out and some of us felt that expenditure by the BHA in this area still exceeded income. The levy was therefore increased to £10 per ceremony. This caused resentment among some officiants, especially in those areas where the network had been well established for some time and was apparently running smoothly. Some individuals were adamantly opposed to the increased levy but others in the same area were able to see the logic of its introduction. As a result, tensions grew within local groups of officiants.

Where an individual has worked hard to establish a local network of officiants and to put in place strong links with funeral directors, he may easily think of the set up as his private fiefdom and resent what he sees as unnecessary central interference. In a few cases, that resulted in relationships becoming strained between the local coordinator and individual officiants with allegations by individuals of failure by the coordinator to allocate ceremonies fairly. To me, and probably to most outsiders, it seems petty and to call for heads to be banged together, but on the other hand, I'm sure that most people could readily think of similar situations. Those who work hard to support an organisation quite often see themselves as having earned the right to determine the way in which things are done long after the circumstances in which they originally operated have changed dramatically. I feel sure that common sense will eventually be applied, especially as the demand for humanist ceremonies is continuing to grow.

My humanist priorities began to change at the BHA Conference in Birmingham in 2003. The final morning included contributions by Roy Brown and Babu Gogineni, respectively President and Executive Director of the International Humanist and Ethical Union (IHEU). I thought that they took a broad view of the problems in the world that are associated with religions that was close to my own concerns about sustainable development. I became a Life Member of IHEU and in the spring of 2004, I was asked to submit my name as a candidate for election as a Vice President of the IHEU. I agreed and at meeting in May 2004 in Kampala, Uganda, although I was unable to attend the meeting, I was elected. At about the same time, my three years as a member of the Executive Committee of the BHA was coming to an end and I decided that I would not seek re-election. I made that decision with some reluctance, but I felt that I was unlikely to be able to make a real contribution to both BHA and IHEU.

Another post-retirement invitation came via a roundabout route soon after our move to Hedley. In the early nineties, I had become

Author's wife, Deborah, with grandchildren Robbie and Philippa Baruch, Farne Islands

friendly with Paul Woolston, a Partner (later Senior Partner), in the Newcastle office of PricewaterhouseCoopers. He had advised Durham County Cricket Club on the preparation of the business plan that was presented to Lords in support of the County's application for first-class status and was a strong supporter of Sunderland AFC. Even before we moved north, Paul occasionally invited me to join him as a guest in the PWC box at Roker Park and after the club moved to the Stadium of Light in 1997, I sometimes joined him there. On one such occasion, Paul said that Professor Caroline Cantley of Northumbria University had asked him to suggest someone with some business experience who might be interested in becoming a Trustee of a charity called Dementia North, of which she was Director. I had seen at first hand the effect of Alzheimer's on my old Chairman, Sir Leonard Millis, over the last year or two of his life and therefore was interested in becoming involved.

Caroline Cantley and Andrew Fairbairn, the Chairman of Dementia North came to Hedley and after our chat I knew that I wanted to help them in their work. Probably most people with dementia are cared for at home and this can obviously place a great strain on the carers, usually family members. The work being done by Dementia North in partnership with the University of Northumbria aimed to help carers to understand the best ways of helping people suffering from dementia, thereby helping both the patient and the carer at the same time. Dementia North is one of several similar charities around the UK and is unusual in operating as a kind of fund-raising arm of Northumbria University enabling the University to access research funding that would not otherwise be available to the University.

As I've learned more about the work being done, I've begun to realise how much is being achieved outside the medical approach to help our understanding of the various forms and stages of dementia. The possibility of becoming totally dependent on others has worried me occasionally for a long time. Therefore, the realisation that much is now being done has been of some comfort to me. The understanding of dementia and improvements in caring is not as sexy as, say, cancer research, but the people working in the field are doing truly vitally important work. Whether they are researchers or carers in care homes or within the family, they are fulfilling a role in our society that is likely to become more and more important as we become ever more successful in controlling the diseases that used commonly to limit our expectation of life.

CHAPTER 14

When I consider how my light is spent (apologies to John Milton)

Music, when soft voices die,
Vibrates in the memory –
Odours, when sweet violets sicken,
Live within the sense they quicken.

Rose leaves, when the rose is dead,
Are heaped for the beloved's bed;
And so thy thoughts, when thou art gone,
Love itself shall slumber on.

Percy Bysshe Shelley,
'*To –: Music, when soft voices die*' 1824

'GROWING OLD GRACEFULLY' has long been a phrase in common use. I've never been quite clear what people mean by it except perhaps in the superficial sense of not wearing clothes that were designed for someone forty years younger. To me, being convinced that this is the only life we have, I can't imagine not wanting to make the most of my life for as long as I continue to possess my faculties. Some people (not many), occasionally question why, when I'm well into my seventies, I continue to rush off to meetings in London or wherever. Trying to help the various organisations with which I'm involved has been one of the key things that has motivated me all my life. That's been true of Laleham Cricket Club through the Royal Institute of Public Health and many other bodies to Newcastle University and the IHEU. I know that everyone doesn't have the opportunities that I've had and I've been fortunate to have them and to have a wife who has understood my motivation and my commitments. I can't imagine a retirement devoted entirely to leisure activities.

On the other hand, I do enjoy my leisure. Being on holiday with Deborah with or without other friends or family, watching cricket or football, walking Floss, our basset-hound, on the beach next to our cottage at Hauxley, visiting the theatre, reading and listening to music at home or in the concert hall all give me enormous pleasure.

But I also need my continuing work with Durham County Waste Management Company, with the Royal Institute of Public Health, with Newcastle University and with Dementia North. My connection with Chopwell Cricket Club counts, I suppose, as leisure but having become President of the club in 2003, I'm now trying to play a small part in helping the club with applications for grants for pitch covers and for cricket nets etc.

Of course, it's possible that I'm fooling myself. Maybe the way in which I've always been driven just demonstrated a need for acceptance and status but I've always been somewhat suspicious of psychiatry, having seen how ineffective it can be. On the other hand, in my time as an operational manager, I usually tried to understand the reasons for the ways in which people behave.

In any case, it really doesn't matter why I want to carry on working in retirement. The genes I inherited from my parents and grand-parents taken with my childhood, schools, university and other parts of the environment of my life made me the way I am. And where the balance lies generally between nature and nurture, I'll leave others to consider, although on reflection, why on earth would anyone be interested?

When I was young, I used to think that I could do anything, both physically and mentally. As I get older, I'm gradually coming to terms with my limitations and with the idea of my mortality. Death itself doesn't worry or frighten me. Having been brought up with a clear understanding that this is the only life I have seems to have helped me to acceptance of the inevitability of death. But I would not want to live on for any significant time after severe impairment of my faculties and would hate any prospect of becoming a burden on Deborah, or indeed anyone else.

I've had a wonderful life. Improvements in society have meant that I've had opportunities that my mother and father never had. I've probably not made quite as much of those opportunities as I might have done, because although I've always been driven to do my best at any one moment, I've never been quite single-minded enough to really reach the top in anything. Shades of my teacher at Stanley Grammar School telling me that I must decide whether I wanted to be a musician, a cricketer or pass my Higher School Certificate!

But I have lived and enjoyed a full life. I've made many, many good friends, had a reasonably satisfying career and played cricket, football and badminton to a decent standard. I've also been able to indulge my love of music by attending concerts and listening to recordings and by playing the piano. On the way, I've achieved a lifelong ambition by buying a Blüthner grand piano similar to the piano on which Arthur Blackburn taught me to play so many years ago, and in 2005 I've started taking piano lessons again after a gap of nearly sixty years. And I have a wine cellar with quite a good selection of claret and burgundy.

Above all, I've been so lucky to meet and marry Deborah and to have three daughters, Wyn, Carole and Jill, each successful in their own way. I also have four talented grandchildren, the eldest of whom, Anna, has as I write this, just completed her third year at Christ Church, Oxford reading medicine, whilst her cousin Philippa has now begun her course at Newcastle University reading politics and economics. Either of them is quite capable of becoming another woman Prime Minister, and their younger cousins Lauren and Robbie will not be far behind.

It's been a long road from Stockton through Pickering Nook Council Junior Mixed School, Stanley Grammar School, The Royal Air Force, and King's College, Newcastle to the water industry and everything else. I plan to carry on for a good many years yet putting pressure on my various pension funds and trying to improve the world. Who knows, there may yet be a sequel to this memoir?

Index